D0771486

The World Since 1900

Sourcebook

Longman Group UK Limited,
Longman House, Burnt Mill, Harlow,
Essex CM20 2JE, England
and Associated Companies
throughout the world

Published in the United States
of America
by Longman Inc., New York

© Longman Group UK Limited
1989

First published 1989

Designed by Ken Brooks
Set in 9/12 Helvetica and 10/12
Ehrhardt Linotron
Produced by Longman Group
(F.E.) Limited
Printed in Hong Kong

ISBN 0 582 00989 8

British Library Cataloguing in Publication Data

Brooman, Josh
  The world since 1900: sourcebook.
  1. World, 1900
  I. Title
  909.8'08

  ISBN 0-582-00989-8

Library of Congress Cataloging in Publication Data

Brooman, Josh.
  The world since 1900: sourcebook / Josh Brooman.
    p.   cm.
  Companion volume to: Twentieth century history / Tony Howarth. 2nd ed. 1987.
  Summary: Describes the political and social changes throughout the world from 1900 to the present day.
    ISBN 0-582-00989-8 : £3.95
  1. History, Modern – 20th century – Juvenile literature.
  [1. History, Modern – 20th century.]   I. Howarth, Tony. Twentieth century history.   II. Title.
  D421.B723 1989
  909'.82 – dc19   88–22957
                                                                    CIP
                                                                    AC

Josh Brooman

The World Since 1900
Sourcebook

Longman

London and New York

Acknowledgements

This book has been compiled as a companion to Tony Howarth's *Twentieth Century History: The World Since 1900*, the second edition of which was revised by Josh Brooman following the death of the author in 1980. The sourcebook can either be used on its own or alongside the textbook which is linked to the BBC series for schools on twentieth century history, *History File*.

We are grateful to the following for permission to reproduce copyright material:
Basil Blackwell Ltd for an extract from *Modern China* by C K Macdonald; Chatto & Windus on behalf of the estates of the author and the editor for an extract from the poem 'Dulce et Decorum Est' from *The Poems of Wilfred Owen* edited by Edmund Blunden; the author's agents for an extract from *Akenfield* by Ronald Blythe; William Collins Sons & Co Ltd for extracts from *The Holocaust* by Martin Gilbert; Columbia University Press for an extract from *The Manchurian Crisis 1931–32: A Tragedy in International Relations* by S R Smith Copyright © 1948 Columbia University Press; Daily Telegraph PLC for an extract from an article by Douglas Brown in *The Daily Telegraph* 1.9.47; André Deutsch Ltd and Little, Brown and Company for extracts from *Khruschev Remembers* by N Khruschev, translated and edited by Strobe Talbott, US Edition Copyright © 1970 by Little, Brown and Company (Inc); Faber & Faber Ltd and Time Books, a division of Random House, Inc for extracts from *The Second American Revolution: A First-Hand Account of the Struggle for Civil Rights* by Anthony Lewis and contributors to the New York Times; the author's agents on behalf of the Trustees of the Mass Observation Archive 1976 for an extract from *Living Through the Blitz* by Tom Harrisson; Grafton Books, a division of the Collins Publishing Group and Monthly Review Foundation for extracts from *Mau Mau from Within* by D L Barnett and K Njama, US Edition Copyright © 1966 Donald L Barnett and Karari Njama; Harrap Ltd and Macmillan Publishing Company, for an extract from *A Year in Upper Felicity* by Jack Chen, US Edition Copyright © 1973 by Jack Chen; the Controller of Her Majesty's Stationery Office for an extract from *Cmnd 6120 (Germany No 2 1939)*; Hodder and Stoughton Ltd and Times Books, a division of Random House, Inc. for an extract from *China: Alive in the Bitter Sea* by Fox Butterfield; Moral Majority Inc, for an extract from the article *Is Our Grand Old Flag Going Down the Drain?*; Oxford University Press for extracts from *Documents on International Affairs 1947–1948* (pub 1952); Time Life Books for extracts from *The British Empire: Revolution Against the Raj* by Michael Edwards © Time-Life International 1972; the University of Exeter for extracts from *Nazism 1919–1945 Vol 2 State, Economy and Society 1933–39* edited by J Noakes and G Pridham.

We have been unable to trace the copyright holders in the following and would appreciate any information that would enable us to do so: *Peace with Horror* by John Barron and Anthony Paul (1977); *North Vietnam: a Documentary* by John Gerassi (1968); the poem 'Prohibition is an awful flop . . .' from *The American Republic Since 1865* Vol 2 (1959) by R Hofstadter, William Miller and David Aaron.

We are grateful to the following for permission to reproduce photographs and other copyright material:
Associated Press, page 103; Bildarchiv Preussicher Kulturbesitz, page 4; Camera Press, page 92 (photo: Jacob Sutton); The Central Zionist Archives, Jerusalem, page 141; Communist Party Library, page 135; John Hillelson, page 77 (photo: Robert Capa); Hulton Deutsch Collection, page 84; Imperial War Museum, pages 7, 8, 17; Library of Congress, Washington, pages 29, 30; News Chronicle, page 53 (John Frost Historical Newspaper Service); Popperfoto, page 152; Punch, page 100; Society for Cultural Relations with USSR, page 75; State Museum in Oświęcim, page 81; Time-Life Picture Agency, page 103 (photo: Edward Clark); Times Newspapers, page 154; UPI/Bettmann Newsphotos, page 109; Trustees of the Victoria & Albert Museum, page 3; Wayland Picture Library, page 38; Wide World Photos Inc, pages 105, 106; The Wiener Library, page 140.

We are unable to trace the copyright holders of the following, pages 60, 99, 144, 151 and would be grateful for any information that would enable us to do so.

Contents

1 Imperial attitudes: the European empires, 1900–14   1

2 The 'Great War': the First World War, 1914–18   7

3 A shaky kind of peace: the Paris Peace Settlement of 1919–20   15

4 'The dawn of a new world': Russia, 1917–24   22

5 Land of liberty? The USA in the twenties   29

6 Depression and New Deal: the USA in the thirties   38

7 The organisation of terror: Hitler's Germany, 1933–45   46

8 The Great Purge: Stalin and the Soviet Union, 1935–38   55

9 Down the road to war: international relations, 1931–39   62

10 People at war: civilians in the Second World War, 1939–45   70

11 Cold War, containment, confrontation: East–West relations after 1945   78

12 The wind of change: African independence movements after 1945   87

13 The jewel in the crown? India, 1900–47   96

14 A thirty-year war: Indo-China, 1945–75   104

15 The Great Society? The USA since 1945   112

16 The USSR without Stalin: the Soviet Union since 1953   120

17 'Liberation': China after 1949   129

18 Conflict in the Middle East: the Arab–Israeli conflict since 1917   138

19 A United Kingdom? Great Britain since 1945   147

To the reader

All the sources in this book have been copied exactly from the books which are named at the side of each extract or picture. The spellings and grammar of the documents have not been changed, so that in some cases unusual expressions occur. No words have been changed, but some have been cut and three dots show where a cut has been made. To make some of the sources easier to understand, difficult or unusual words have been starred and their meaning explained in the right-hand margin.

1   Imperial attitudes: the European empires, 1900–14

At the start of this century, over half the world was ruled by eight small nations in Western Europe. The British, French and Belgians, the Germans and the Dutch, the Italians, Spanish and Portuguese had spent the previous fifty years competing with each other to colonise any unclaimed part of the globe. By 1900 they had imposed their laws, their methods of government, their economic systems and, in many places, their religious beliefs on more than half the human race.

Today, fewer than a million people still live under European colonial rule, for only a few small outposts of the eight European empires remain. The twentieth century has seen a steady reversal of Europe's colonising process; and the struggle of colonial peoples to gain their independence has been one of the most remarkable developments of the past fifty years. To understand this important story, it is worth trying to look inside the minds of the people who imposed European rule on half the world.

Cecil Rhodes, Great Britain's famous empire-builder, said in 1877:

A We happen to be the best people in the world, with the highest ideals of decency and justice and liberty and peace, and the more of the world we inhabit, the better it is for humanity.

Cecil Rhodes, *Confession of Faith*, 1877.

Not all humanity may have agreed with Rhodes's opinion, but many of the British did. By 1900 the Union Jack flew over a quarter of the world's land surface. Every year, thousands of English, Scots, Irish and Welsh bought one-way tickets to colonies in all five continents. Whatever their reasons for emigrating – to be missionaries, to make money, to escape the law, for example – these people shared many assumptions and attitudes about their country's empire. Some of those attitudes can be glimpsed in this extract from *The Settlers' Guide* of 1914, a handbook describing the British colonies for the benefit of intending and newly-arrived settlers:

B *British East Africa*, the only British colony actually traversed by the equator, lies south of Italian Somaliland and north of German East Africa and fronts the Indian Ocean with a seaboard of about 450 miles. . . .

The *population* in 1911 consisted of 3,256 whites – 2,071 males and 1,185 females, and 2,399,607 natives and coloured.

The *native races* are numerous and of varied origin; in the Nyanza Province the *Kavirondo* predominate and supply the best farm and plantation labourers of the Protectorate. . . . They are remarkable for the curious habit of wearing no clothes whatever. In the Naivasha Province the *Masai* are the most important tribe. They are essentially a fighting race . . .; as their tribal customs debar them from working and barter, their ultimate future must offer a difficult problem. Kenia and Ukamba Provinces are peopled by the *Ki-kuyu* . . . with a temperamental as opposed to a caste prejudice against work. The *Wa-kamba* . . . have a curious aptitude for controlling machinery. The *Swahili* . . . is an excellent agriculturalist, a good servant, generally clean in his person and altogether of a higher type than the inland tribes. The *East Indian* population is considerable; some 25,000 coolies of a low type were employed in the construction of the Uganda Railway, and the majority remained in the country on completion of the line. . . .

IMMIGRATION – British East Africa is eminently suited to the small capitalist who is prepared to make his home there. Nowhere else, in so small an area, are so many varieties of occupation, agricultural and pastoral, open to the newcomer.

Applicants for land must satisfy the Authorities that they are possessed of not less than £400 capital, and no white man without means is allowed to proceed up country except to a situation.

A class to whom British East Africa should strongly appeal is that represented by the Public Schoolboy . . . firstly because he will find that a large percentage of the settlers are men of his own class, and secondly because his upbringing should fit him to control the natives whose labour is essential to all and every undertaking.

From G. Gordon Brown and G. Noel Brown (eds.), The Settlers' Guide. Greater Britain in 1914: A Summary of the Opportunities offered by the British Colonies to Settlers of All Classes, Simpkin, Marshall, Hamilton, Kent & Co., 1914.

---

1 Describe in your own words the writer's attitude towards the 'native races' of British East Africa.
2 Using the information on '*population*' and 'IMMIGRATION', describe in your own words the kind of person who might have wanted to settle in British East Africa.
3 How might a member of one of the 'native races' described in source B have replied to Cecil Rhodes's claim in source A?
4 How useful is source B as evidence of British attitudes to the Empire in the early 1900s?

If such attitudes seem outrageous today, we must remember that people then could not easily escape them. Imperial attitudes were reflected in the press and the cinema, in schoolbooks and children's comics, in music-hall shows and on cigarette cards, in church hymns and popular songs, and in a hundred other ways. Source C shows one way in which people could, without knowing it, acquire imperial attitudes. It is an extract from a school geography textbook published in Britain in 1902, and widely used up to the 1930s.

C [Before colonisation] . . . the natives of Australia . . . were among the most miserable of men. They roamed nearly naked, and were ignorant of everything except the chase. The explanation of their degraded condition lies in the arid climate of Australia. . . . Their great poverty led them to practise vices like cannibalism and the murder of the sick and helpless.

From A. J. Herbertson and F. L. D. Richardson, Man and his Work: An Introduction to Human Geography, A. & C. Black, 1902.

---

1 How can school textbooks help to shape the ideas and attitudes of young people?
2 Describe in your own words the attitude of the author of source C towards the 'natives of Australia'.
3 Bearing in mind that the book from which source C is taken was used widely in British schools up to the 1930s, do you think this is a useful source of evidence about British attitudes towards colonisation? Explain your answer.

Source D shows another way in which people could acquire imperial attitudes from the everyday things of life. It is an advertisement for electric light bulbs published in Britain around 1900.

D

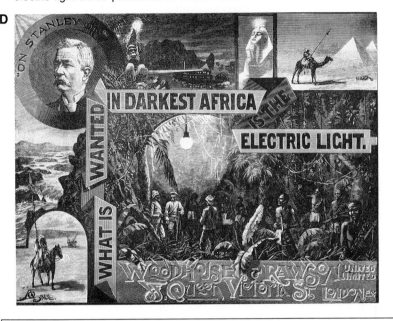

1 What impression does the advertisement give of (a) Africa, (b) African people, and (c) European people in Africa?
2 What point do you think the artist was trying to make about Woodhouse and Rawson Ltd's products? Why do you think the artist used an African setting to make this point?
3 Do you think it is fair to use this advertisement as evidence of British people's attitudes towards their African empire in 1900? Explain your answer.

As Cecil Rhodes's comment in source A suggests, the British generally believed that their empire was a very superior one; not only bigger than all the others, but also better governed, more just and more free. Moreover, the British generally believed that the other empires, particularly those of Belgium and Germany, were barbaric and crude in comparison to theirs. Sources E and F are typical of the widespread belief that the Germans and Belgians treated the native populations of their colonies with great cruelty. Source E is a report by E. Alexander Powell, a member of the American consular service in Egypt, after a tour of German East Africa in 1913:

E There is not a town in German East Africa where you cannot see boys of from eight to fourteen years shackled by chains running from iron collar to iron collar, and guarded by soldiers with loaded rifles, doing the work of men under a deadly sun. Natives with bleeding backs are constantly making their way into British and Belgian territory with tales of maltreatment by German planters, while stories of German tyranny, brutality and corruption – of some instances of which I myself was a witness – were staple topics of conversation on every club veranda and steamer's deck along these coasts.

E. Alexander Powell, *The Last Frontier*, 1913.

Source F is a letter from Roger Casement, British Consul to the Belgian Congo, to the Belgian Vice-Governor of the Congo, in September 1903.

F [The] population is supposed to be free and protected by excellent laws; those laws are nowhere visible; . . . force is everywhere. Well-nigh each village has its gang of armed and unscrupulous ruffians quartered upon it; and where they are not actively present, the shadow of the public forces of this government . . . serves as an ever-impending reminder of the doom facing the recalcitrants.

Communities that fail to satisfy the unceasing demands made upon them, either for india-rubber, food stuffs, or some other local want of the European establishments in their neighbourhood, are then said to be 'in a state of revolt', and the entire population, men women and children are treated worse than the worst criminals in any country I have knowledge of.

Quoted in L. H. Gann and Peter Duignan (eds.), *Colonialism in Africa, 1870–1960*, vol. 1, Cambridge University Press, 1969.

---

1 What do sources E and F reveal about German and Belgian rule in their African colonies?
2 Do you have any reason to doubt the reliability of either source E or source F? Explain your answer.

There are usually two sides to a story, and so the Germans had their own stories to tell about the brutality of other colonial powers. The leading culprits, in their eyes, were the British. This German cartoon, published in 1909, shows a British settler in Africa squeezing profits out of a native African who has been drugged with religion and made drunk with whisky.

Source: Staatsbibliothek, Berlin.

G

A German historian, Heinrich von Treitschke, wrote in 1903 that:

H . . . the hypocritical English people, with the bible in one hand and a pipe of opium in the other, possesses no redeeming qualities. . . . The English have a commercial spirit, a love of money which has killed every sentiment of honour and every distinction of right and wrong.

Quoted in David Heald, 'How Others Saw Us', in *The British Empire*, Time-Life Books, 1973.

---

1 What criticisms of the British Empire are made by sources G and H?
2 How are the criticisms made in G and H similar to those made in E and F? How do they differ?
3 Compare source A with sources G and H. How can you explain the great difference of opinion in these sources about the nature of British colonial rule?

Finding fault with each others' imperial attitudes was not confined to people of different nationalities. People of the same nationality sometimes disagreed strongly with each other about their empire. One such disagreement was recorded by a British army officer in his diary, after a heated conversation with the British High Commissioner in Kenya:

I He amazed me with his views on the future of East Africa. He envisaged a thriving colony of thousands of Europeans with their families, the whole of the country . . . divided up into farms: the whole of the Rift Valley cultivated or grazed, and the whole country. . . .under white settlement. He intends to confine the natives to reserves and use them as cheap labour on farms. I suggested that the country belongs to Africans and that their interests must prevail over the interests of strangers. He would not have it; he kept on using the word 'paramount' with reference to the claims of Europeans. I said that some day the African would be educated and armed; that would lead to a clash. Eliot thought that that day was far distant and that by that time the European element would be strong enough to look after themselves; but I am convinced that in the end the Africans will win.

From Colonel T. Meinertzhagen, *Kenya Diary 1902–1906*, Oliver & Boyd, 1957.

---

1 To what extent are the German criticisms of the British Empire in sources G and H borne out by the British High Commissioner's views in source I?
2 Judging by what you have read, whose attitudes do you think were more typical of British people at the time – those of the High Commissioner or the writer of the diary? Explain your answer.

But whatever disagreements they had on the subject of empire, Europeans tended to agree on one thing: that their empires were rapidly spreading 'civilisation' to the most backward areas of the world. As Lord Curzon, a former Viceroy of India, put it in 1907 in a speech on 'The True Imperialism':

J Wherever this Empire has extended its borders, there misery and oppression, anarchy and destitution, superstition and bigotry, have tended to disappear, and have been replaced by peace, justice, prosperity, humanity and freedom of thought, speech and action. . . . Imperialism is animated by the supreme idea, without which it is only as sounding brass and a tinkling cymbal, viz. the sense of sacrifice and duty.

Speech in Birmingham, December 1907, quoted in The Earl of Ronaldshay, *The Life of Lord Curzon*, vol. 3, Ernest Benn Ltd., 1928.

In contrast, the native peoples of the colonies had very different opinions about the activities of the European colonisers. Source K comes from the memory of Vwa Mak, a Nigerian villager. Speaking in 1977, aged 86, Vwa Mak recalled the day in 1905 when the British first came to Riyom, his village:

K The white man that came to Riyom, came with many soldiers. By then we had already heard that some white things were setting villages on fire. . . . When the white man was not allowed to see the chief, he grew annoyed and set the chief's house on fire. We, having no knowledge of matches, thought he produced fire from his fingers. It was then we knew these white things were exceptional and really thought they were not human beings because no human being could be so wicked.

Vwa Mak of Riyom, recorded by the Plateau History Project, University of Jos, Nigeria, in July 1977. Quoted in Elizabeth Isichei, *A History of Nigeria*, Longman, 1983.

---

1 Compare sources J and K. How might Lord Curzon have tried to explain the behaviour of the soldiers in source K?

2 Does source K prove that Lord Curzon's view of 'The True Imperialism' was inaccurate? Explain your answer.

---

1 Using the sources in this chapter as evidence, describe the attitudes towards their empires that were common among Europeans at the start of this century.

2 Which of the sources in this chapter do you think are most useful as evidence of European imperial attitudes at the start of the century?

3 If you were researching this subject in greater detail, what other sources of evidence would you look for?

2 The 'Great War': the First World War, 1914–18

The First World War of 1914–18 began as a good old-fashioned war. Soldiers in smart uniforms marched off to fight what their generals promised would be a short war – 'over by Christmas' at the latest, they said. The families they left at home cheered them on their way, certain that they were going to fight in a good cause. And even if they could not actually say what that cause was, it did not really matter: the politicians, the generals, the newspapers, the next-door neighbours, all seemed to know.

Over the next four years and three months the 'Great War', as people began to call it, grew into a global war, the first of its kind. Nearly fifty million men wearing the uniforms of thirty different countries found themselves fighting for the cause. Ten million of them were killed and twice that many were wounded or crippled. And by the time it was over in 1918 nobody was really much clearer about why the war had been fought: no one could say with confidence why ten million men had died. Some people even said that it had all been a pointless waste of human life.

The sources in this chapter have been chosen to illustrate some of the reasons why people were so keen to go to war in 1914 and why, by 1918, many of them had turned against it.

When Britain declared war on Germany on 4 August 1914, the German Imperial Chancellor said that 'just for a scrap of paper, Great Britain is going to make war on a kindred nation, which desires nothing better than to be friends with her'.

That 'scrap of paper' was the Treaty of London which Britain had signed seventy-five years before, declaring that Belgium was an independent and 'perpetually neutral' state, and promising to protect her independence. In fact, there were other reasons for declaring war on Germany: Britain did not want a hostile power dominating the other side of the 'English' Channel; Britain did not want to see France, with whom she was friendly, wiped out as a great power; and Britain did not want Germany to grow any stronger as a naval power. But the defence of 'Brave Little Belgium' was the issue on which British public opinion was united, even though the promise to defend her had been made three quarters of a century before. This British postcard of 1914 sums up many British people's feelings about going to war over 'a scrap of paper'.

A

Source: Imperial War Museum.

"A SCRAP OF PAPER"

1 What is represented by (a) the bulldog bitch, and (b) her puppies?
2 Suggest what the flags around the picture represent.
3 Explain the meanings of the words 'Treaty', 'For Honour' and 'A Scrap of Paper' in the picture.
4 What message do you think the artist was trying to put across?

Thousands of propaganda posters were produced in 1914 as part of every country's war effort. In many cases, their aim was to persuade men to enlist in their country's army. Source B is a British recruiting poster issued in 1914:

B

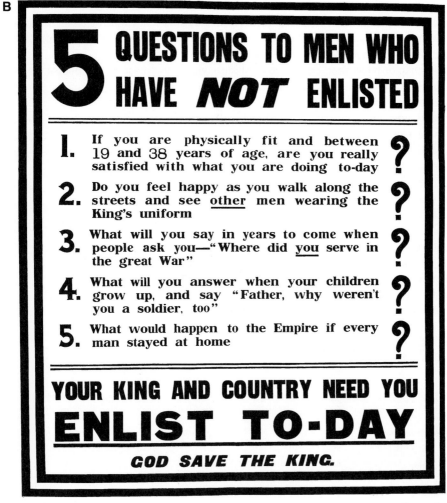

5 QUESTIONS TO MEN WHO HAVE *NOT* ENLISTED

1. If you are physically fit and between 19 and 38 years of age, are you really satisfied with what you are doing to-day **?**

2. Do you feel happy as you walk along the streets and see other men wearing the King's uniform **?**

3. What will you say in years to come when people ask you—"Where did you serve in the great War" **?**

4. What will you answer when your children grow up, and say "Father, why weren't you a soldier, too" **?**

5. What would happen to the Empire if every man stayed at home **?**

YOUR KING AND COUNTRY NEED YOU
ENLIST TO-DAY
GOD SAVE THE KING.

Source: Imperial War Museum.

1 Explain how this poster was intended to persuade men to join the army.
2 What similarities and what differences as propaganda are there between sources A and B?

Many young men enlisted in the army as a result of this kind of propaganda, but once they reached the front they found they couldn't explain what they were fighting for. In his autobiographical novel *Her Privates We* (1930), Frederic Manning described how men could get themselves into this situation:

C 'Well, what the 'ell did you come out for?' asked Madeley.
   Weeper lifted up a large, spade-like hand with the solemnity of one making an affirmation.
   'That's where th'ast got me beat lad,' he admitted. 'When a saw all them as didn't know any better'n we did joinin' up, an' a went walkin' out wi' me girl on Sundays, as usual, a just felt ashamed. An' a put it away, an' a put it away, until in the end it got me down. I knew what it'd be, but it got the better o' me, an' then, like a bloody fool, a went an' joined up too. A were ashamed to be seen walkin' in the streets, a were.'

From F. W. Manning, *Her Privates We*, Peter Davies, 1930.

1 Why did Weeper join the army?
2 Does the fact that source C is an autobiographical novel affect its value as historical evidence? Explain your answer.

In every country that went to war in 1914, the pressure on young men to enlist was enormous. In Austria-Hungary, the country which started the conflict with an attack on neighbouring Serbia, a young Communist named Ernst Fischer witnessed the following scenes, which he described in his memoirs sixty years later.

D The war that began in 1914 ... revealed its nature to me through two experiences. Awkward young soldiers were being pelted with flowers by women and girls. The streets of Graz were full of excited people marching towards the Sudbahnhof*. Their patriotism reeked of alcohol. Over and over came the roar: 'Death to all Serbs! Long Live the Emperor! Down with Traitors!' Outside the station, in the middle of a knot of howling, screaming, insane people, a man was dragged to the ground, trampled upon, torn limb from limb. 'A Serbian spy!' went the cry from one mouth to another as the remains of a human being were retrieved from the murderous mob.

* railway station

Ernst Fischer, *An Opposing Man*, Allen Lane, 1974.

1 Suggest why young women and girls were pelting 'awkward young soldiers' with flowers?
2 For what two reasons, according to Ernst Fischer, were the crowds in Graz so excited?
3 Why do you think the crowd tore the alleged spy 'limb from limb'?

Like Ernst Fischer, many soldiers who survived the 'Great War' later wrote memoirs of their experiences. The memoir in source E is rather different: it is by an English farm worker named Leonard Thompson, and was tape-recorded by a writer, Ronald Blythe, in 1967 when Leonard Thompson was seventy-one years old.

E When the farmer stopped my pay because it was raining and we couldn't thrash, I said to my seventeen-year old mate, 'Bugger him. We'll go off and join the army.' It was March 4th 1914. . . .

In my four months' training with the regiment I put on nearly a stone in weight and got a bit taller. They said it was the food but it was really because for the first time in my life there had been no strenuous work. I want to say this simply as a fact, that village people in Suffolk in my day were worked to death. It literally happened. It is not a figure of speech. I was worked mercilessly. I am not complaining about it. It is what happened to me.

We were all delighted when war broke out on August 4th. I was now a machine-gunner in the Third Essex Regiment. A lot of boys from the village were with me and although we were all sleeping in ditches at Harwich, wrapped in our greatcoats, we were bursting with happiness. We were all damned glad to have got off the farms. I had 7s. a week and sent my mother half of it. If you did this, the government would add another 3s.6d. so my mother got 7s.

All the trouble with the village fell behind us now. I was nineteen and off to the Dardanelles. . . . I had two boys from the village with me. We'd heard a lot about France, so we thought we'd try Turkey. The band played on the banks of the river as we pulled out of Plymouth and I wondered if we would ever come home again. We were all so patriotic then and had been taught to love England in a fierce kind of way. The village wasn't England. England was something better than the village.

We arrived at the Dardanelles and saw the guns flashing and heard the rifle-fire. . . . The first things we saw were big wrecked Turkish guns, the second a big marquee. It didn't make me think of the military but of the village fêtes. . . . We unlaced it and rushed in. It was full of corpses. Dead Englishmen, lines and lines of them, and with their eyes wide open. We all stopped talking. I'd never seen a dead man before and here I was looking at two or three hundred of them. It was our first fear. Nobody had mentioned this. I was very shocked. I thought of Suffolk and it seemed a happy place for the first time. . . .

We set to work to bury people. We pushed them into the sides of the trench but bits of them kept getting uncovered and sticking out, like people in a badly made bed. Hands were the worst; they would escape from the sand, pointing, begging, even waving! There was one we all shook when we passed, saying 'Good morning' in a posh voice. Everybody did it. The bottom of the trench was springy like a mattress because of all the bodies underneath. At night, when the stench was worst, we tied crêpe round our mouths and noses. This crêpe had been given to us because it was supposed to prevent us being gassed. The flies entered the trenches at night and lined them completely with a density that was like moving cloth. We killed millions by slapping our spades along the trench walls but the next night it would be just as bad. We were all lousy and we couldn't stop shitting because we had caught dysentery. We wept, not because we were frightened but because we were so dirty.

We didn't feel indignant against the government. We believed all they said, all the propaganda. We believed the fighting had got to be done. We were fighting for England. You only had to say 'England' to stop any argument.

From Ronald Blythe, *Akenfield: Portrait of an English Village*, Allen Lane, 1969.

---

1 Why did Thompson join the army, and why was he happy when the War began?
2 What do you think Thompson and his mates had heard about France, and why should this make them want to 'try Turkey'?
3 Which of his experiences in the Dardanelles seem to have upset Thompson the most?
4 What sort of propaganda do you think prevented Thompson from feeling 'indignant against the government'?
5 How many years after the start of the War were sources D and E written? In what ways might this affect their usefulness as evidence of people's attitudes to the War at the time?

Soldiers who fought in the front line of the trenches had to cope with the constant dread of being blown to pieces by high-explosive shell fire, of being gassed, or shot, or mutilated in a dozen ways. Yet relatively few soldiers refused to fight. One soldier who did refuse was Siegfried Sassoon, an officer in the Royal Welsh Fusiliers, who had won a Military Cross for gallantry one year earlier. He gave his reasons in a letter to his commanding officer on 15 June 1917:

F I am making this statement as an act of wilful defiance of military authority, because I believe that the War is being deliberately prolonged by those who have the power to end it. I am a soldier, convinced that I am acting on behalf of soldiers. I believe that this War, upon which I entered as a war of defence and liberation, has now become a war of aggression and conquest. I believe that the purposes for which I and my fellow soldiers entered upon this war should have been so clearly stated as to have made it impossible to change them, and that, had this been done, the objects that actuated us would now be obtainable by negotiation. I have seen and endured the sufferings of the troops, and I can no longer be a party to prolong these sufferings for ends which I believe to be evil and unjust. I am not protesting against the conduct of the War, but against the political errors and insincerities for which the fighting men are being sacrificed. On behalf of those who are suffering now I make this protest against the deception which is being practised on them; also I believe I may help to destroy the callous complacency

with which the majority of those at home regard the continuance
of agonies they do not share, and which they have not sufficient
imagination to realise.

From Rupert Hart Davis (ed.),
Siegfried Sassoon Diaries 1915–1918,
Faber, 1983.

---

1 What arguments might Sassoon have used to support his view that the War was 'a war of defence and liberation' when it began in 1914?
2 List the objections that Sassoon had against any more fighting.
3 What do you think Sassoon hoped to achieve by making this statement?
4 As a result of this protest, Sassoon was sent to a psychiatric hospital in Scotland. Why do you think he was not court-martialled and shot for disobeying orders?

Siegfried Sassoon was a poet as well as a soldier, one of a group of war poets who used verse to describe the horror and suffering of modern warfare. Probably the greatest of the war poets was Wilfred Owen, who wrote this poem early in 1917 after experiencing a German poison gas attack.

G Dulce et decorum est

Bent double, like old beggars under sacks,
Knock-kneed, coughing like hags, we cursed through sludge,
Till on the haunting flares we turned our backs,
And towards our distant rest began to trudge.
Men marched asleep. Many had lost their boots,
But limped on, blood-shod. All went lame, all blind;
Drunk with fatigue; deaf even to the hoots
Of gas-shells dropping softly behind.

Gas! GAS! Quick, boys! – An ecstasy of fumbling,
Fitting the clumsy helmets just in time,
But someone still was yelling out and stumbling
And floundering like a man in fire or lime. –
Dim through the misty panes and thick green light,
As under a green sea, I saw him drowning.

In all my dreams before my helpless sight
He plunges at me, guttering, choking, drowning.

If in some smothering dreams, you too could pace
Behind the wagon that we flung him in,
And watch the white eyes writhing in his face,
His hanging face, like a devil's sick of sin;
If you could hear, at every jolt, the blood
Come gargling from the froth-corrupted lungs,
Bitter as the cud
Of vile, incurable sores on innocent tongues, –

My friend, you would not tell with such high zest
To children ardent for some desperate glory,
The old Lie: Dulce et decorum est
Pro Patria mori*.

It is sweet and proper to die for your country

Wilfred Owen, *Poems*, Chatto & Windus, 1920.

---

1 Briefly describe in your own words the events depicted in this poem.
2 What message do you think Wilfred Owen was trying to convey?
3 Could Wilfred Owen have put across this message as effectively in prose? Explain your view.
4 How useful are war poems like this as evidence of people's attitudes to the 1914–18 War?

By 1918, most well-informed people had come to realise the full horror of the War and there was general agreement that the 'Great War' must be a 'war to end all war'. This sense of revulsion against war is seen in source H, a note written in 1919 by Winston Churchill, who was First Lord of the Admiralty from 1911–15, Minister of Munitions in 1917, and Secretary of State for War in 1919:

H All the horrors of all the ages were brought together, and not only armies but whole populations were thrust into the midst of them. The mighty educated states involved conceived – not without reason – that their very existence was at stake. Neither peoples nor rulers drew the line at any deed which they thought could help them to win. Germany, having let Hell loose, kept well in the van of terror; but she was followed step by step by the desperate and ultimately avenging nations she had assailed. Every outrage against humanity or international law was repaid by reprisals – often of a greater scale and of longer duration. No truce or parley mitigated the strife of the armies. The wounded died between the lines: the dead mouldered into the soil. Merchant ships and neutral ships and hospital ships were sunk on the seas and all on board left to their fate, or killed as they swam. Every effort was made to starve whole nations into submission without regard to age or sex. Cities and monuments were smashed by artillery. Bombs from the air were cast down indiscriminately. Poison gas in many forms stifled or seared the soldiers. Liquid fire was projected upon their bodies. Men fell from the air in flames, or were smothered often slowly in the dark recesses of the sea. The fighting strength of armies was limited only by the manhood of their countries. Europe and large parts of Asia and Africa became one vast battlefield on which after years of struggle not armies but nations broke and ran. When all was over, Torture and Cannibalism were the only two expedients that the civilised, scientific, Christian States had been able to deny themselves; and they were of doubtful utility.

From *Churchill Papers*, quoted in R. S. Churchill and Martin Gilbert, *Winston S. Churchill, vol. 4*, Heinemann, 1966.

1 Make a list in your own words of 'the horrors of all the ages' which Churchill mentions in source H. Which of them belonged to past ages, and which were horrors invented in the twentieth century?
2 Why, according to Churchill, did the War become so horrific?
3 Bearing in mind that Churchill was a member of the British government during the War, helping to lead the British war effort, why do you think he wrote this note criticising all the states which had taken part in it?

1 Using sources A to E as evidence, make a list of reasons why many people were enthusiastic about the War in 1914. Which of those reasons seem to have been most important?
2 Using sources F to H as evidence, make a list of reasons why many people stopped supporting the War after 1914.

3 A shaky kind of peace: the Paris Peace Settlement of 1919–20

On 18 January 1919, 1,037 delegates from twenty-seven countries assembled in Paris to begin making peace treaties with the Central Powers they had defeated in the First World War. One of them, Woodrow Wilson, President of the United States, said in his opening speech:

A In a sense, this is the supreme conference in the history of mankind, for more nations are represented here than were ever represented in such a conference before, and the fortunes of the entire world are involved.

Quoted in Charles T. Thompson, *The Peace Conference Day by Day*, Brentano's, New York, 1920.

For the next five months the peacemakers in Paris laboured to make a set of treaties which, they hoped, would provide the world with lasting peace. But even before their signatures had dried on the first one, the Treaty of Versailles, some of the peacemakers were voicing doubts about their prospects of success. In a newspaper article published in Britain on 28 June 1919, Jan Smuts, a South African delegate, wrote:

B I feel that in the Treaty we have not yet achieved the real peace to which our peoples were looking. . . .

There are territorial settlements which in my humble judgement will need revision. . . .

There are punishments foreshadowed, over most of which a calmer mood may yet prefer to pass the sponge of oblivion.

There are indemnities* stipulated, which cannot be enacted without grave injury to the industrial revival of Europe.

* fines

The Smuts Papers, Box 9. No. 5, quoted in J. C. Smuts, *Jan Christian Smuts*, Cassell and Co., 1952.

And Marshal Foch, the French Commander of the Allied Armies in 1918, put it more bluntly. Speaking on 28 June 1919, the day when the Treaty of Versailles was signed, he said:

C This is not peace. It is an armistice for twenty years.

Quoted in Peter Vansittart, *Voices from the Great War*, Jonathan Cape, 1981.

Smuts and Foch both proved correct in their predictions: the Treaty did not achieve the 'real peace' that people were looking for, and a second world war broke out exactly twenty years later. So what went wrong? Why were the peacemakers voicing such grave doubts about their work so soon after they had signed their Treaty?

One of the reasons why the peacemakers were dissatisfied with their work can be seen in sources D, E and F: each one had very different aims in making peace, and different ideas about how it should be done. The French, to start with, wanted security against any future attack by Germany, so for them the peace settlement had to ensure that Germany would never again be strong enough to make war. Furthermore, the French wanted the Germans to pay for the destruction caused by four years of warfare on French and Belgian soil. The intensity of French feelings can be seen in this 'Memorandum of the French Government to the Peace Conference' dated 26 February 1919:

D Hopes, without certainty, cannot suffice to those who suffered the aggression of 1914. Hopes, without certainty, cannot suffice to Belgium, victim of her loyalty to her pledged words, punished for her loyalty by invasion, fire, pillage, rape and ruin. Hopes, without certainty, cannot suffice France, invaded before the declaration of war, deprived in a few hours . . . of 90 per cent of her iron ore and 86 per cent of her pig-iron; France, who lost 1,351,000 killed, 734,000 crippled, 3,000,000 wounded and 438,000 prisoners martyred in German prisons, who lost 26 per cent of her mobilised manpower and 57 per cent of her soldiers under 31 years of age – the most productive part of the nation – who saw a quarter of her productive capital wiped out, the systematic destruction of her industrial districts in the north and in the east, the captivity of her children, her women and her girls.

Quoted in Etienne Mantoux, *The Carthaginian Peace*, Oxford University Press, 1946.

---

1 Explain the meaning of the phrase 'Hopes, without certainty, cannot suffice . . .' at the start of each sentence in source D.
2 What do you think the French government hoped to achieve by sending this memorandum to the Peace Conference?
3 In what ways does the memorandum make its point by appealing to (a) the reader's emotions, and (b) historical facts? Quote from the memorandum to support your answer.

The British government, however, realised that Britain had nothing to gain by treating Germany as harshly as the French wanted. Winston Churchill, Secretary of State for War, explained why this was so in a speech to the Aldwych Club in London on 11 April 1919:

E All the information I receive from military sources indicates that Germany is very near collapse. All my military advisers, without exception, have warned me that the most vital step we ought to take immediately . . . is to provide Germany with food and raw materials.

　　The situation in Germany is grave. The Socialist Government of Scheidemann and Ebert and Noske is tottering, and if it falls no one knows what will take its place. If Germany sinks into Bolshevist anarchy she will no doubt be skinned alive, and not only will there be no indemnity, but we shall ourselves be impoverished, and our trade revival will be paralysed by the increasing disorder and ruin of the world.

The Times, 12 April 1919.

---

1 In your own words, give three reasons why Churchill opposed the idea of treating Germany harshly.
2 How does Churchill's view of Germany in 1919 differ from the British Empire Union view in source F opposite?

Many British people agreed whole-heartedly with the French point of view. Millions of them had family and friends recently buried on the battlefields of France. Popular slogans like 'Hang the Kaiser!' and 'Make Germany Pay!' reflected their hatred of Germany in 1919, as did this poster:

F

Source: Imperial War Museum.

1 Describe the impression of German soldiers created in the first four scenes on this poster.
2 What point was the artist trying to make with the fifth scene of a German salesman?
3 What do you think was the overall message that the artist was trying to put across?
4 How useful do you consider this poster as evidence of British attitudes towards Germany in 1919?

The aims of the American government were already well known when the Peace Conference began. President Woodrow Wilson had described them in January 1918, in a speech to the US Congress:

G What we demand in this war ... is nothing peculiar to ourselves. It is that the world be made fit and safe to live in; and particularly that it be made safe for every peace-loving nation which, like our own, wishes to live its own life, determine its institutions, be assured of justice and fair dealing by the other peoples of the world as against force and selfish aggression. All the peoples of the world are in effect partners in this interest, and for our own part we see very clearly that unless justice be done to others it will not be done to us. The programme of the world's peace is therefore our programme.

From *Congressional Record vol LVI.*

---

1 How does (a) the tone, and (b) the content of source G differ from the tone and content of sources D and E?

In the Fourteen Point peace programme which he went on to read to the Congress, Wilson put great emphasis on giving the right of self-determination to peoples living under the rule of foreign empires. This meant, for example, allowing the Polish citizens of Germany, Austria-Hungary and Russia to form their own independent, self-governing nation out of land belonging to those empires. The idea of self-determination, however, was to cause disagreement even among the American delegates at the Peace Conference. One of them, Robert Lansing, wrote in his diary on 30 December 1918:

H The more I think about the President's declaration as to the right of 'self-determination', the more convinced I am of the danger of putting the idea into the minds of certain races. It is bound to be the basis of impossible demands on the Peace Congress and create trouble in many lands.

What effect will it have on the Irish, the Indians, the Egyptians, and the nationalists among the Boers? Will it not breed discontent, disorder and rebellion ...?

The phrase is simply loaded with dynamite. It will raise hopes which can never be realised. It will, I fear, cost thousands of lives. In the end it is bound to be discredited, to be called the dream of an idealist who failed to realise the danger until too late. ... What a calamity that the phrase was ever uttered! What misery it will cause!

From Robert Lansing, *The Peace Negotiations: A Personal Narrative,* Constable and Co., 1921.

---

1 Explain in your own words what the phrase 'self-determination' means.
2 Suggest why Lansing thought that giving the right of self-determination to 'certain races' would lead to 'impossible demands' on the Peace Conference.
3 Write a brief reply to Lansing's criticisms as if you were Woodrow Wilson.

There were many other differences of aim among the peacemakers, particularly over the subject of making Germany pay reparations and the question of disarming Germany. But differences of aim among the peacemakers were not the only defect of the Versailles settlement. Another important defect was Article 231 of the Treaty, the 'War Guilt Clause', which laid all the blame for starting the First World War on Germany and her allies. The German reaction to this part of the Treaty was stronger than to any other. Count von Brockdorff Rantzau, leader of the German delegation in Paris, made this statement about Germany's war guilt after reading the Treaty for the first time:

I Gentlemen. . . . We are under no illusion as to the extent of our defeat and the degree of our want of power. We know that the power of German arms is broken. We know the extent of the hatred which we encounter here, and we have heard the passionate demand that the vanquishers shall make us pay as the vanquished, and shall punish those worthy of punishment.

It is demanded of us that we confess ourselves to be the only ones guilty of starting the war. Such a confession in my mouth would be a lie. We are far from declining any responsibility that this great war of the world has come to pass. But we deny that Germany and its people were alone guilty.

We have not come here to belittle the responsibility of the men who waged the war politically and economically, and to deny any crimes which may have been committed. We repeat the declaration made in the German Reichstag: 'Wrong has been done to Belgium' and we are willing to repair it.

But in the manner of making war, Germany is not the only guilty one. I will not answer reproaches with reproaches, but I ask you to remember, when reparation is demanded, I ask you to remember the Armistice. It took you six weeks before the Armisitice was arranged, and six months before we came to know your conditions of peace. The hundreds of thousands of non-combatants who have perished since the 11th November, when the Armistice was concluded, by reason of the continued blockade, have been killed with cold deliberation. . . . Think of that, gentlemen, when you speak of guilt and punishment.

Quoted in Charles T. Thompson, *The Peace Conference Day by Day*, Brentano's, New York, 1920.

---

1 Does Winston Churchill's statement in source F agree with the claim in source I that the Allied blockade of Germany after the 1918 Armistice killed many non-combatants 'with cold deliberation'?

2 After listening to the speech in source I, Woodrow Wilson said, 'This is the most tactless speech I have ever heard. It will set the whole world against them.' Why do you think he thought this?

Despite their misgivings, the Germans eventually agreed to sign the Treaty of Versailles: the alternative to signing was an Allied invasion of their country.

The opening paragraphs of the Treaty said a great deal about the difficulties that had been involved in making it:

J The United States of America, the British Empire, France, Italy and Japan,

These Powers being described in the present Treaty as the Principal Allied and Associated Powers,

Belgium, Bolivia, Brazil, China, Cuba, Ecuador, Greece, Guatemala, Haiti, The Hedjaz, Honduras, Liberia, Nicaragua, Panama, Peru, Poland, Portugal, Roumania, the Serb-Croat-Slovene State, Siam, Czecho-Slovakia and Uruguay,

These powers constituting with the Principal Powers mentioned above the Allied and Associated Powers,

of the one part;

And Germany,

of the other part. . . .

From The Treaty of Peace between the Allied and Associated Powers and Germany, and other Treaty Engagements, signed at Versailles, June 28th, 1919, H.M.S.O., 1920.

---

1 How many Allied and Associated Powers signed the Treaty?
2 What did these Powers have in common?
3 What do you think they did not have in common?
4 How might these differences have made the task of writing a satisfactory Treaty difficult?

With so many Allied Powers involved, and with so many issues to be settled, the Treaty of Versailles turned out to be immensely long – more than two hundred closely printed pages containing over four hundred separate articles. Much of it dealt directly with Germany, taking away land from her, reducing her armed forces, arranging for the payment of reparations, and so on. But many of the articles also dealt with the individual grievances of the Allies. Article 246 of the Treaty of Versailles is an example of this:

K Within six months from the coming into force of the present Treaty, Germany will restore to His Majesty the King of the Hedjaz the original Koran of the Caliph Othman, which was removed from Medina by the Turkish authorities and is stated to have been presented to the ex-emperor William II.

Within the same period Germany will hand over to His Britannic Majesty's Government the skull of the Sultan Mkwawa which was removed from the Protectorate of German East Africa and taken to Germany.

From The Treaty of Peace between the Allied and Associated Powers and Germany and other Treaty Engagements, signed at Versailles, June 28th, 1919, H.M.S.O., 1920.

---

1 To whom do you think the 'Koran of the Caliph Othman' and the 'skull of the Sultan Mkwawa' were valuable?
2 Is it fair to say that articles like this brought unnecessary complications into an already complex treaty? If so, how better could such issues have been dealt with?

As we have seen, the Treaty of Versailles came under fire as soon as it was signed. Some said it was too harsh, others that it was too mild. Some said it was unjust, others that it was unwise. A few said it was impractical and would never work, especially with regard to its insistence that Germany pay reparations to the Allies. The debate about the Treaty, which continued for the following twenty years, still raises important questions today.

1 Is it fair to say, judging by the sources in this chapter, that the peacemakers of 1919 lacked clear and agreed aims?

2 (a) Was the idea of German 'war guilt' a necessary part of the Treaty?

 (b) Is it possible to say that a whole nation is guilty of wicked acts, and must therefore be punished?

 (c) Was it possible, in the circumstances of 1919, to avoid the issue of German 'war guilt'?

3 Was it possible to make a treaty involving so many countries satisfactory to every one of them?

4 'The dawn of a new world': Russia, 1917–24

In 1919 a party of American government officials visited Russia to find out how the world's first Communist state was faring. With the group was a journalist named Lincoln Steffens. On his return to the United States, Steffens was asked what Communist Russia was like. He replied: 'I have been over into the future – and it works.'

Less than a year later, on 26 February 1920, the Russian Communist newspaper *Pravda* had this to say about the condition of the country: 'The workers of the towns and of some of the villages choke in the throes of hunger. The railroads barely crawl. The houses are crumbling. The towns are full of refuse. Epidemics spread and death strikes to the right and to the left. Industry is ruined.'

What had Lincoln Steffens seen to make him so enthusiastic? And what had happened to produce the ghastly scenes described by *Pravda* in 1920? Russia in 1919–20 was clearly a land of many strange and vivid contrasts, producing different pictures in the eyes of each observer. The sources in this chapter illustrate some of those remarkable contrasts, and help to explain why intelligent observers could produce such different descriptions of the same scene.

Immediately after seizing power in November 1917, the Bolsheviks showed what they intended to do with Russia in a series of new laws and decrees. Many of the new laws shocked and puzzled Russians as well as foreigners. These extracts from the early decrees give an idea of their scope:

A *8 November 1917. Decree on Land.*
The landlord's right to the land is hereby abolished without compensation.... The right of private ownership of land is abolished forever. Land cannot be bought, sold, leased, mortgaged, or alienated in any manner whatsoever. All lands ... become the property of the people, and are turned over for the use of those who till them.

8 November 1917. Decree on Peace.
The Workers' and Peasants' Government, created by the revolution of November 6–7 ... proposes to all warring peoples and their governments to begin at once negotiations leading to a just and democratic peace.

11 November 1917. Decree on the Hours of Work.
The working time or the number of working hours in a day is the time when a workman is obliged to be in the factory for the performance of work. The working time should not exceed eight working hours a day and forty-eight hours a week.

13 November 1917. Decree on Social Insurance.
1. Insurance for all wage workers without exception....
2. Insurance to cover all forms of disability, such as illness, injury, invalidism, old age, maternity, widowhood, orphanage as well as unemployment.
3. The total cost of the insurance to be borne by the employer.

15 November 1917. Decree on the Rights of the Peoples of Russia to Self-Determination.
1. Equality and sovereignty of all the peoples of Russia.
2. The right to free self-determination of peoples even to the point of separating and forming independent states.
3. Abolition of each and every privilege or limitation based on nationality or religion.
4. Free development of national minorities and ethnographic groups inhabiting Russian territory.

18 November 1917. Decree on the Transfer of Power and the Means of Production to the Toilers.
Comrades – Workers, Soldiers, Peasants, All Toilers! . . . Remember that you are now running the government. . . . Your Soviets* are from now on all-powerful and decisive organs of government.

* councils of soldiers and workers

23 November 1917. Decree abolishing class distinctions.
All classes and class distinctions are abolished. . . . All estates (noble, merchant, commoner, peasant, etc.), titles (prince, count, etc.) and designations of civil ranks (privy councillor, state councillor, etc.) are abolished, and in their places the inhabitants of Russia are to have one name common to all – citizens of the Russian Republic.

27 November 1917. Decree Nationalising Banks.
All existing banks . . . are to become a part of the State Bank.

29–30 December 1917. Decrees on the Army.
The full power within any army unit is to be in the hands of its soldiers' committees and Soviets. . . . All commanders are to be elected. . . . Sovnarkom* hereby decrees 1. To do away with all ranks and titles from the rank of corporal to that of general. . . . 3. To do away with saluting; 4. To do away with all decorations and signs of distinction.

* the government

From James Bunyan and H. H. Fisher (eds.), *The Bolshevik Revolution, 1917–1918: Documents and Materials*, Stanford University Press, 1965.

31 December 1917. Decrees abolishing Church Marriage and establishing Civil Marriage and Divorce. . . .

---

1 Make a list of the kinds of people you think were likely to (a) welcome these new laws and decrees, and (b) dislike them.
2 How might European or American visitors to Russia have reacted to these decrees? Explain your answer.

New laws were made not only at national level by the government, but also on a local level by Soviets – the councils of workers and soldiers mentioned in source A. One such law is described here by Helen Clarke, an English governess to a Russian family living in the city of Kharkov. This extract from her memoirs, written in 1921, concerns a train journey she took in the summer of 1918, during which local Bolshevik soldiers searched the passengers' luggage. In the extract, the soldiers have just found bullets for a revolver in a young man's luggage.

B No one was allowed to carry a revolver. If it were found after its existence had been denied, the penalty was instantaneous death. They shook their fists at him and shouted 'For God's sake, give us the revolver or we will shoot you where you stand. What are these cartridges for if you have no revolver?'

It was a terrifying moment. Our little children began to cry quietly, and the elder ones to say their prayers and cross themselves. The Bolsheviks had also made a law that no one should be allowed to have more than two of every garment: two shirts, two pairs of boots, two pairs of trousers, and so on. While this argument was proceeding in connection with the revolver, searching was in progress among the other passengers' luggage. All at once there was a lull in the tumult. It had been discovered that one of the passengers had two pairs of trousers in his bag! One pair he was wearing and two in his bag! This important discovery came as a godsend to the poor young man with the cartridges. The ruffians threw themselves upon the unfortunate owner of the nether garments. . . . The poor man was very much distressed, and begged to be allowed to keep his garments, but all to no avail. They were torn from his trembling hands amidst yells of fury and with this prize the ruffians left us.

From the unpublished memoirs of Helen Clarke, quoted in Harvey Pitcher, When Miss Emmie was in Russia: English Governesses before, during and after the October Revolution, John Murray, 1977.

---

1 Why do you think the local Bolsheviks made a law that no one should have more than two of every item of clothing?
2 What impression does Helen Clarke create of (a) her fellow passengers, and (b) the Bolshevik soldiers?
3 How might a supporter of the Bolsheviks have reported this story differently?

The new laws made by the government and by local Soviets brought about many profound changes in Russian society. One of these changes is described here by Louise Bryant, an American Communist who visited Russia for six months in 1918.

C Russia, in my imagination, had always been 'holy' Russia, and it was surprising to go there and find it so apparently unholy. The shrines along the streets loomed blackly, forgotten and unlit. The churches for the most part were silent and deserted. . . .

Russians are deeply religious, like the Irish or the Italians, and they always will be religious. But the church today in their minds is all knit with the Tsar and the old regime and is naturally absolutely discredited. Once the Little Father* was divine, now he is only a poor exile with all his weaknesses exposed. . . .

* nickname of the Tsar

An incident which I witnessed in Petrograd in December illustrates an amusing new resentment among the people for the superior feeling of the priests. I was riding on a street car one morning when a priest climbed aboard. He refused to pay his fare, saying he was a man of God and therefore exempt. Immediately the passengers became excited. They were mostly peasants and they began to argue hotly. A man of God, they claimed, was no different from any other man – all were equal since the revolution. But the priest was stubborn and not until the crowd threatened to take him to the Revolutionary Tribunal did he consent to pay, grumbling.

From Louise Bryant, *Six Months in Red Russia*, William Heinemann, 1918.

1 Why, according to Louise Bryant, did profoundly religious Russians become hostile to the church?
2 How does the street car incident show that Bolshevik rule was already having big effects on Russia?
3 Is it possible to tell from source C whether Louise Bryant supported or opposed the changes she saw?

The Russians who had most to lose from Communist rule took up weapons to fight the Bolsheviks. From 1918 to 1920 former nobles, landowners, churchmen, nationalities wanting their independence, anarchists, Socialist Revolutionaries, and all sorts of other 'White' groups made war on the 'Reds' – the Bolsheviks. This civil war brought ruin and suffering to millions of ordinary people who got caught between the Reds and the Whites. This extract from the diary of Colonel Drozdovsky, a White officer, shows how badly people could suffer in the Russian Civil War:

D The head of the column arrived at Vladimirovka about 5.00 pm. . . . Then the mounted platoon entered the village, met the Bolshevik committee and put the members to death, after which they demanded the surrender of the murderers and the instigators in the torturing of the four Shirvan men. . . . Our charge was so speedy and unexpected that no culprit had time to escape. . . . They were delivered to us and executed on the spot. The two officers concealed by the people of Vladimirovka were guides and witnesses. After the execution, the houses of the culprits were burned and the whole male population under forty-five whipped soundly, the whipping being done by the old men. The people of this village are so brutal that when these officers had been arrested the Red Guards* were not thinking of murdering them, but the peasants, their women and even children insistently demanded their death. It is characteristic that some women were anxious to save their relatives from whipping at the price of their own bodies – what more! . . . Then the population was ordered to deliver without pay the best cattle, pigs, fowl, forage and bread for the whole detachment, as well as the best horses. All this they kept bringing over until nightfall. . . . 'An eye for an eye.' The whole village set up a howl.

* Bolshevik soldiers

From James Bunyan and H. H. Fisher (eds.), *The Bolshevik Revolution, 1917–1918: Documents and Materials*, Stanford University Press, 1965.

1 Why did Colonel Drozdovsky's column invade the village?
2 Why do you think the White soldiers punished the whole male population of the village and made the villagers give them all their best animals and food?

The civil war wrecked the Russian economy. The greatest damage was done to food supplies, as this article in the Russian newspaper *Rossiya* on 4 March 1920 shows:

E Here are the prices on the Petrograd market last week. Bread 450 rubles per lb.; flour 500–700 rubles per lb.; meat 550–650 rubles per lb.; pork 720 rubles per lb.; salt 300 rubles per lb.; butter 2,000–3,200 rubles; groats* 500–700 rubles per lb.; makhorka* 5,000–6,000 rubles per lb.; matches from 75–100 rubles per box; cigarettes 11–13 rubles each; yellow soap 700–800 rubles per lb. A single fare on a tram costs 6 rubles. In spite of these prices salaries are comparatively low. A woman typist gets 3,200 rubles per month, without food. A nurse receives 2,600 rubles per month and a soldier's one day ration.

* coarsely ground grain

* low-grade tobacco

From Martin McCauley (ed.), *The Russian Revolution and the Soviet State, 1917–21: Documents*, Macmillan, 1975.

---

1 Who, judging by source F, was better off, the typist or the nurse? Explain your answer.
2 Using the prices in source F, draw up a shopping list for a month's meals for the typist earning 3,200 rubles per month.

Food shortages grew worse in 1921 and developed into a full-scale famine. The famine, the Red Terror, the civil war, and the disruption of the economy created widespread hatred of the Bolsheviks. In March 1921 the sailors at Kronstadt naval base near Petrograd rose in revolt against them. They explained their reasons for revolt in this statement:

F We joined the Communist Party to work for the good of the people and stand for the help of the workers and peasants. Therefore at the present hard time which our country is surviving, when all our efforts have to be turned to the struggle with misery, cold and hunger, we state that we do not stand for power, but for the interest of the workers. . . .

The worker, instead of becoming the master of the factory, became a slave. He can neither work where he would like to, nor can he reject work that is beyond his physical strength. Those who dare to say the truth are imprisoned to suffer in the torture-cells of the Cheka*, or are shot. . . .

* secret political police

Therefore, as honest men, standing for the defence of the interest and rights of the workers, we declare that we call ourselves the Temporary Revolutionary Committee, which takes the task of creating Soviets entirely from the proletarian masses.

We are fighting for the liberation of the workers.

Long live the Soviet Power, the true defender of the workers.

From *News of the Temporary Revolutionary Committee of Sailors, Red Army Soldiers and Workers of the City of Kronstadt*, 3 March, 1921.

---

1 In your own words, describe the sailors' complaints.
2 How useful do you consider source F as evidence of the problems facing Russian people in 1921?

Lenin said later that the Kronstadt Rising was a 'flash that lit up reality better than anything'. After crushing the rising with great severity, Lenin admitted the need for a radical change in government policy. His New Economic Policy (NEP) of 1921 provided that change. The NEP relaxed the government's control of the economy and allowed peasants to trade their surplus crops. Some of the results can be seen in this extract from the diary of a Russian academic, Pitrim Sorokin, who was expelled from Russia in 1922:

G The New Economic Policy, forced upon the Communists, began to have a revivifying effect on the country. As in a fairy tale, the dead land seemed to come to life. . . . Shops and stalls, private offices and workshops, very poor and primitive at first, were opened. Wonderful it was to see exhibited in shop windows bread and meat, butter and vegetables. Just to enter without any permission, without any waiting in long queues, and to buy the little that one could afford gave the most intense happiness. Those who have never known starvation . . . cannot even faintly imagine how happy we were now.

Little by little Petrograd began to assume the outward aspect of a European city. People were repairing their houses, taking some care of their dress and appearance. The marks of desolation and death which had rested on us like a pall for two years, by September 1922, had almost entirely been obliterated. Luxurious hotels, restaurants with signs 'Everything as before', tram cars running, droshkies*, theatres and movies, decently dressed people, such was the outward appearance of the town. . . .

* horse-drawn cabs

From Pitrim Sorokin, *Leaves from a Russian Diary*, Hurst and Blackett, 1925.

---

1 What does source G tell you about conditions in Petrograd before the introduction of the New Economic Policy?
2 What effects did NEP have on daily life, according to source G?

For about a million Russians, however, NEP had little or no effect. They were the children who had lost their parents or who had been separated from their families during the civil war and famine. This report by a Finnish businessman, Boris Cederholm, shows what life was like for some of these orphans in 1924:

H Petrograd, and still more Moscow, astonish the newly-arrived foreigner by their swarms of hooligans and uncared-for children. . . .

The colonies for juvenile offenders and the ordinary prisons are filled to the brim with young criminals. I myself . . . saw dozens of little girls engaged in prostitution in broad daylight, and continually saw small boys of 12 or 13 taking cocaine.

I was returning from Tsarskoe Selo late one evening by the suburban railway. The compartment was crammed full of ragged boys of 12 or under, who conversed on sexual subjects with a frank cynicism. The guard, coming through the carriage, made a sign for me to leave the compartment, and suggested I should move to another carriage.

'It's dirtier there, but its safer,' he said. 'Those boys are a pack of ruffians; they wouldn't stop at murder. They all take cocaine.'

In the alleys of Petrograd and Moscow, child criminals in regular gangs fall upon any at all decently dressed woman and extort money from her by threatening to pour acids on her face or to bite her in order to infect her with venereal disease. A lady of my acquaintance was set upon at 11 o'clock one night near the Alexandrovsky market by a crowd of small boys and girls, who threatened to let loose typhus germs, specially preserved in a small box, on her fur coat. She ransomed herself for five rubles and thought she had got off very lightly.

From Boris Cederholm, *In the Clutches of the Tcheka* (translated by F. H. Lyon), Allen and Unwin, 1929.

---

1 What social problems does source J show still existed in Russia in 1924?

Louise Bryant, whose observations we read in source C, wrote that:

I felt as if I were continually witnessing events which might properly come centuries later. I was continually startled and surprised. . . . I who saw the dawn of a new world can only present my fragmentary and scattered evidence to you with a good deal of awe. I feel as one who went forth to gather pebbles and found pearls.

From Louise Bryant, *Six Months in Red Russia*, William Heinemann, 1918.

---

1 In general, what picture of Russia emerges from sources A to H in this chapter? Quote from the sources to support your answer.

2 Judging by what you have read in this chapter, why do you think Louise Bryant (source I) felt she had seen the 'dawn of a new world' in 1918?

3 How might Louise Bryant's views (source I) have changed if she had stayed for six years rather than six months?

5   Land of liberty? The USA in the twenties

The scene in this poster and the message that it carries are dear to many American hearts. For most of the thirty million immigrants who had arrived in the USA by 1920, this view of the Statue of Liberty as they sailed into New York Harbour was their first glimpse of their new country. And one of the things that had tempted many of them to make that voyage was the belief that they would find liberty in the USA: the liberty to live freely and equally in a democratic society; freedom of speech and belief; freedom from repressive government and heavy taxation; above all, the opportunity to make a new start in life. In the words of the American Declaration of Independence, 'Life, Liberty and the Pursuit of Happiness' were basic rights which every American could expect to enjoy.

Some features of US society in the 1920s show that many Americans were able to enjoy 'Life, Liberty and the Pursuit of Happiness' to the full. But there were also some ugly features of American society which suggest that there was a dark side of the American dream. The sources in this chapter illustrate some of those features, light and dark, and ask how far the American people still experienced the 'thrill of American liberty' in the 1920s.

A A poster for United States Government war bonds, 1917

Source: Library of Congress, Washington, DC.

By 1920 the USA was a 'nation of nations'. With over a million immigrants arriving in her ports each year, the USA was home for 106 ethnic groups, with more languages, cultures and religions than any other nation in the world. Increasingly, however, native-born white Americans were demanding a halt to this flood of immigration. One of them, Senator Heflin of Alabama, explained why in a speech in 1921:

B The steamship companies haul them over to America, and as soon as they step off the decks of their ships, the problem of the steamship companies is settled, but our problem has but begun – bolshevism, red anarchy, black-handers and kidnappers, challenging the authority and integrity of our flag. . . . Thousands come here who never take the oath to support our constitution and to become citizens of the United States. They pay allegiance to some other country while they live upon the substance of our own. They fill places that belong to the loyal wage-earning citizens of America. . . . They are of no service whatever to our people. . . .

Quoted in J. T. Patterson, *America in the Twentieth Century: A History*, Harcourt Brace, 1976.

---

1 Summarise Senator Heflin's reasons for wanting to stop immigration into the USA.
2 How might the view of immigrants on a steamship as shown in source A differ from that described by Senator Heflin?

Senator Heflin got support for his views in the US Congress. An Immigration Act in 1921 limited immigration in any year to 3 per cent of the numbers of each nationality that had been living in the USA in 1910. The aim of this 3 per cent quota was to fix the ethnic balance of the population at its current level. The quota was tightened by two more Immigration Acts in 1924 and 1929. The 1929 Act fixed the quota according to the national origins of the US population in 1920. The reasoning behind that quota can be seen in this drawing which appeared in an American magazine in 1921:

C

Source: Library of Congress, Washington, DC.

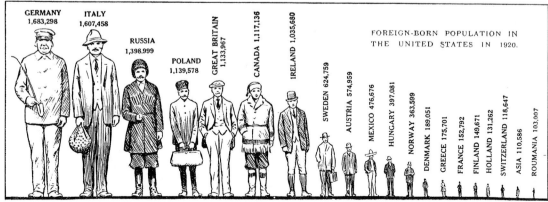

GERMANY 1,683,298 · ITALY 1,607,458 · RUSSIA 1,398,999 · POLAND 1,139,578 · GREAT BRITAIN 1,133,967 · CANADA 1,117,136 · IRELAND 1,035,680 · SWEDEN 624,759 · AUSTRIA 574,959 · MEXICO 476,676 · HUNGARY 397,081 · NORWAY 363,599 · DENMARK 189,051 · GREECE 175,701 · FRANCE 152,792 · FINLAND 149,671 · HOLLAND 131,262 · SWITZERLAND 118,647 · ASIA 110,586 · ROUMANIA 103,007

FOREIGN-BORN POPULATION IN THE UNITED STATES IN 1920.

1 Judging by source C, from which parts of the world did the foreign-born population of the USA mostly come? Which parts of the world had contributed fewest immigrants by 1920?
2 Using sources A, B and C as evidence, list the kinds of immigrant which the US authorities wanted (a) to exclude, and (b) to encourage in the 1920s.

As a result of the Immigration Acts of the 1920s, foreign immigration slowed to a trickle. However, the fall in immigration was matched by a sharp increase in internal migration, especially of black people from the southern states to the industrial cities of the north. Some of the reasons for their migration to the north can be seen in this article published in a black American newspaper in 1921:

D Look around at your cabin, look at the dirt floor and the windows without glass! Then ask your folks already up north about the bathrooms with hot and cold water . . . the steam heat and the glistening hardwood floors which down home you only see when you polish them. . . . What chance has the average [black] to get these things down home? And if he does get them how can he be sure but that some night some poor cracker* will get his gang together and come round and drive him out? . . . Step on a train and ride for a day and a night to freedom. . . . Your nickel is worth as much as the other fellow's nickel in the [northern] streetcars and you sit wherever you can find a seat. . . . You tip your hat to no man unless you desire to do so.

* white man

Quoted in J. C. Furnas, *Great Times: an Informal Social History of the United States, 1914–1929*, G. P. Putnam's Sons, 1974.

1 What does source D reveal about the conditions of life of black people in the American South in the 1920s?
2 How does source D suggest that black people in the American South suffered from racial discrimination?

So many white Americans were alarmed by the presence of black people and immigrants in their midst that around five million of them joined the Ku Klux Klan, an organisation which aimed to control ethnic and national minority groups. The basic aims of the Ku Klux Klan can be seen in this extract from its rule book.

E 1. Is the motive prompting you to be a Klansman serious and unselfish?
2. Are you a native-born, white, gentile* American?
3. Are you absolutely opposed to and free of any allegiance of any nature to any cause, government, people, sect or ruler that is foreign to the United States of America?
4. Do you believe in the tenets of the Christian religion? . . .
5. Do you believe in and will you faithfully strive for the eternal maintenance of white supremacy?

* non-Jewish

Quoted in R. Coughlan, 'Konklave in Kokomo', in Isabel Leighton (ed.), *The Aspirin Age*, Penguin, 1964.

Members of the Ku Klux Klan were ready to go to any lengths to achieve their aims, as this extract from a newspaper report suggests. It concerns a man accused of murdering a white woman in the southern state of Georgia:

F The negro was taken to a grove, where each one of more than five hundred people, in Ku Klux ceremonial, had placed a pine knot* around a stump, making a pyramid to the height of ten feet. The negro was chained to the stump and asked if he had anything to say. Castrated and in indescribable torture, the negro asked for a cigarette, lit it and blew the smoke into the faces of his tormentors.

    The pyre was lit and a hundred men and women, old and young, grandmothers among them, joined hands and danced around while the negro burned. A big dance was held in a barn nearby that evening in celebration of the burning, many people coming by automobile from nearby cities to the gala event.

* branch

From *The Washington Eagle*, quoted in Daniel Snowman, *America Since 1920*, Heinemann Educational Books, 1978.

---

1 Using sources E and F as evidence, give a detailed description of the kind of person who was likely to belong to the Ku Klux Klan.
2 Try to explain the behaviour of the crowd in source F.
3 Suggest how it was possible for this event to take place without being halted by the police.
4 Does the writer of source F seem to have approved or disapproved of what he/she saw? Explain your answer.

Cruelty and intolerance were provoked not only by skin colour and nationality in the 1920s: people's political views could also get them into trouble if they were considered to be 'radical', a word used to describe anybody on the left wing of politics – Socialist, Communist or Anarchist. This point was made by Mrs Katherine Fullerton Gerould in a letter to *Harper's Magazine* in 1922:

G America is no longer a free country in the old sense; and liberty is, increasingly, a mere rhetorical figure. . . . No thinking citizen, I venture to say, can express in freedom more than a part of his honest convictions. I do not of course refer to convictions that are frankly criminal. I do mean that everywhere, on every hand, free speech is choked off in one direction or another. The only way in which an American citizen . . . can preserve any freedom of expression is to choose the mob that is most sympathetic to him, and abide under the shadow of that mob.

Quoted in F. L. Allen, *Only Yesterday: An Informal History of the Nineteen-Twenties in America*, Penguin, 1938.

Two men who had no 'mob' to protect them were Italian anarchists – Nicola Sacco and Bartolomeo Vanzetti. They were tried in 1920 for a murder which they denied committing and, despite only the flimsiest evidence against them, were found guilty. During the trial, Prosecutor Katzmann made much of their anarchist beliefs, while Judge Thayer was heard referring to them out of court as 'dagos' and 'sons of bitches'. Seven years of appeals failed to reverse the verdict, and they were executed by electric chair in 1927. In his last statement to the court, Vanzetti summed up his feelings about the case:

H Yes. What I say is that I am innocent. . . . In all my life I have never stole and I have never killed and I have never spilled blood. That is what I want to say. And it is not all. . . . You see it is seven years that we are in jail. What we have suffered no human tongue can say, and yet you see me before you, not trembling, you see me looking in your eyes straight, not blushing, not changing colour, not ashamed or in fear. . . .

We were tried during a time that has now passed into history. I mean by that, a time when there was hysteria of resentment and hate against the people of our principles, against the foreigner, against slackers, and it seems to me – rather I am positive, that both you and Mr Katzmann has done all what it were in your power to work out, in order to agitate still more the passion of the juror, the preju-dice of the juror, against us. . . .

I am suffering because I am a radical and indeed I am a radical; I have suffered because I was Italian and indeed I am an Italian; I have suffered more for my family and for my beloved than for myself; but I am so convinced to be right that if you could execute me two times, and if I could be reborn two other times, I would live again to do what I have done already. I have finished. Thank you.

From Henry Steele Commager (ed.), *Documents of American History*, Appleton-Century-Crofts, 1962.

---

1 Why, according to Vanzetti in source H, were he and Sacco found guilty seven years earlier?
2 Judging by what he said and how he said it, why do you think Vanzetti failed to persuade the jury he was innocent?
3 In what way does source H support the views of Mrs Gerould in source G?
4 Does the fact that source H was Vanzetti's final statement to the court, and that he knew he was going to die, make it more or less reliable as evidence?

One group of Americans with strong views became so influential that the United States Constitution was amended to incorporate their views. The Eighteenth Amendment to the Constitution, passed in 1919, banned all Americans from making, selling or even transporting alcoholic drinks. This began a thirteen-year period of 'Prohibition' in which the USA was officially 'dry' as far as alcohol was concerned. Some of the views of those who wanted Prohibition can be seen in source I, a poster put up by the Nashville Tennessee chapter of the Anti-Saloon League:

I Bolshevism flourishes in wet soil. Failure to enforce Prohibition in Russia was followed by Bolshevism.

Failure to enforce Prohibition HERE will encourage disrespect for law and INVITE INDUSTRIAL DISASTER.

Radical and Bolshevist outbreaks are practically unknown in states where Prohibition has been in effect for years. Bolshevism lives on booze.

Quoted in John Kobler, *Ardent Spirits: The Rise and Fall of Prohibition*, Michael Joseph, 1974.

---

1 What criticisms might be made of the argument in source I?
2 Judging by what you have read so far in this chapter, why do you think many people found this argument plausible?

Within weeks of the start of Prohibition in 1920, it became clear that the government was going to have difficulty in enforcing the ban on alcohol. Illegal bars known as speakeasies sprang up in every town and city, and drinkers found hundreds of ways to evade the new law. Source J shows just one of those ways. It is an extract from the sales talk of a young saleswoman in a New York store, demonstrating how to use the product she was marketing – 'The Brick of Bacchus', a block of concentrated grape juice.

J You dissolve the brick in a gallon of water and it is ready to be used immediately.

Do not place the liquid in this jug and put it away in the cupboard for 21 days, because then it would turn to wine.

Do not stop the bottle with this cork containing this patented red rubber siphon hose, because that is necessary only when fermentation is going on.

Do not put the end of the tube into a glass of water, because that helps to make the fermenting liquor tasty and potable*.

Do not shake the bottle once a day because that makes the liquor work.

* drinkable

Quoted in John Kobler, *Ardent Spirits: The Rise and Fall of Prohibition*, Michael Joseph, 1974.

Prohibition was also hard to enforce because the criminals of America's big cities found they could make fantastic profits by trading in illegal 'booze'. The connections between crime and alcohol were explained in an interview given in 1973 by a former gangster, 'Barefoot' Rafer Dooley.

K I began running whisky across the border into California. It wasn't as complicated then as it later turned out to be. For a small stipend the guard would look the other way, and you just drove your pickup truck past him.

I organised a bunch of constituents in Los Angeles. I made contact there again with my brother Ben. He's going much stronger than I am, so he fit me in with some of his operations which consisted of hijacking whisky. . . .

At this time, if I'm not exaggerating, there were about ten mobs in Chicago. There was the Irish North Side mob under Deanie O'Banion, the O'Connell mob on the West Side, Joe Saltis and Frankie McErlane on the South Side – oh, dear God, never has there been such tough guys. The North Side mob gave me and my constituents, about twenty-five of them, a district, an allocation, five blocks square. This was our reward for faithful service in the past. With it went the right to distribute beer and whisky. Of course, you had to protect your territory. You couldn't call for help. If you couldn't handle yourself, you lost it. . . .

It was a nightclub district, full of bars, handbooks*, crap games, gambling joints. It seemed as though every wise-guy heist* artist, mechanic, con man and burglar gravitated to our district. . .

*betting shops
*robbery

I met muscle with muscle trying to defend my equity, and I got hurt. I was shot several times. . . .

They say crime don't pay. You tell that to the real hierarchery of crime and they'll laugh theirselves into nervous hysteria. It don't pay only if you're apprehended. If the venture succeeds, like when me and my constituents were distributing liquor on the North Side, it pays fine, very fine indeed.

Quoted in John Kobler, *Ardent Spirits: The Rise and Fall of Prohibition*, Michael Joseph, 1974.

In 1931 a verse appeared in the *New York World*, summing up the problems involved in enforcing Prohibition:

L Prohibition is an awful flop.
  We like it.
It can't stop what it's meant to stop.
  We like it.
It's left a trail of graft and slime,
It's filled our land with vice and crime,
It don't prohibit worth a dime,
  Nevertheless, we're for it.

Quoted in R. Hofstadter, William Miller and Daniel Aaron, *The American Republic Since 1865*, Prentice-Hall, 1959.

---

1 Using sources J, K and L as evidence, make a list of reasons why Prohibition was difficult to enforce.
2 According to source K, how did Prohibition encourage crime and violence?

Liberty may have been missing from the lives of many Americans, particularly those who happened not to be white, Anglo-Saxon or conservative in their views. But for millions of others, the USA in the twenties provided the kind of economic freedom that the rest of the world could only dream about. As President Calvin Coolidge said in December 1928, in a speech to the US Congress:

M The great wealth created by our enterprise and industry, and saved by our economy, has had the widest distribution among our own people, and has gone out in a steady stream to serve the charity and business of the world. The requirements of existence have passed beyond the standards of necessity into the region of luxury. Enlarging production is consumed by an ever increasing demand at home and an expanding commerce abroad. The country can regard the present with satisfaction and anticipate the future with optimism.

Quoted in Ernest R. May, *Boom and Bust, 1917–32*, Time-Life Books, 1964.

Part of the 'region of luxury' mentioned by Coolidge in source M can be glimpsed in the table below. Produced by a research team in the University of California in 1931, it shows the average yearly spending of three social and income groups in the San Francisco Bay area.

N

Item	Wage earner, family of five	Clerk, family of five	Professional, family of four
Total	$1,631.81	$2,175.19	$6,085.36
Food	507.84	677.64	891.12
Clothing	225.87	339.97	672.19
Husband	61.22	95.32	194.64
Wife	64.37	111.36	320.73
Boy, 11 years	45.13	54.21	79.42
Girl, 5 years	29.43	43.19	77.40
Boy, 2 years	25.72	35.89	. . . .
Rent	336.00	396.00	1,380.94
House operation	199.30	262.69	923.84
Fuel, light, heat	80.42	90.86	192.00
Replacement, furniture	52.68	79.21	229.15
Other items	66.20	92.62	502.69
Miscellaneous	362.80	498.89	2,217.27
Savings	. . . .	. . . .	360.00
Life insurance	65.00	130.00	260.00
Medical and dental care	75.00	75.00	275.00
Church and charity	18.00	18.00	110.00
Gifts	22.50	22.50	112.50
Organisation dues	. . . .	. . . .	36.00
Entertaining guests at home	22.52	22.60	116.60
Theatre and concerts	6.00	12.00	34.00
Movies	22.56	22.56	11.28
Other commercial amusements	10.00	10.00	20.00
Radio upkeep	6.00	7.00	8.00
Excursions	15.00	. . . .	. . . .
Vacation	. . . . . .	52.38	125.00
Automobile	. . . .	. . . .	416.27
Carfare	45.00	60.00	40.00
School supplies	5.00	5.00	5.00
Daily paper	9.00	9.00	13.80
Periodicals and books	2.00	4.00	22.00
Music lessons	. . . .	. . . .	96.00
Tobacco	13.00	18.00	54.00
Haircut and shaving	23.68	27.46	36.12
Cosmetics	2.54	3.39	5.70
Incidentals	. . . .	. . . .	60.00
Total	362.80	498.89	2,217.27

From *Recent Social Trends in the United States; Report of the President's Research Committee on Social Trends*, Vol 2, McGraw-Hill 1933

And Coolidge's message to Congress was supported by another Republican, Herbert Hoover, shortly to succeed Coolidge as President. Hoover declared in 1928:

O We in America today are nearer to the final triumph over poverty than ever before in the history of any land.

Quoted in Ernest R. May, *Boom and Bust, 1917–32*, Time-Life Books, 1964.

---

1 How far does source N support Coolidge's view in source M that American wealth 'has had the widest distribution among our own people'? Quote from the figures to support your answer.
2 How far do these figures support Hoover's view in source O that Americans were close to 'the final triumph over poverty'? Again, quote from the figures to support your answer.

Using sources A to O in this chapter as evidence, explain:
1 Why the USA was still renowned as a 'land of liberty' in the 1920s.
2 Why the liberty of many Americans was in fact very restricted.

6 Depression and New Deal: the USA in the thirties

The Great Depression of 1929 to 1934 was the worst economic slump of the twentieth century. In the USA it put fifteen million people out of work, drove millions from their homes, and brought hunger to more than a quarter of the population. Ever since, the Great Depression has been a byword for the misery and hardship that mass unemployment creates.

It is remarkable, then, that many Americans, both at the time and since, denied that it was happening. Many others who admitted that there was a depression denied that it was serious or that it would last long. These people also argued that the US government should not get too closely involved in helping the victims of the Depression, saying that people without work could, and should, take care of themselves.

For much of the 1930s, American politics were dominated by arguments between those who wanted strong government action to overcome the Depression and those who believed that the government should not interfere in the economic life of the country. These two views are still debated today, and not only in the United States. The issues at stake in the argument are illustrated by the sources in this chapter. We will begin by looking at the Depression through the eyes of its victims.

In the USA in the 1930s there was no national system of unemployment benefits, and in many states there was no local system either. Most people without work therefore had to rely on other people's charity for at least some of their needs. One of the most vivid images of the Great Depression was of 'breadlines' – long queues of hungry people shuffling towards makeshift counters to receive free bread and soup from local charity groups. Source A shows a 'soup kitchen' opened in Chicago by an unlikely giver of charity – Al Capone, America's most notorious gang leader, and Chicago's 'Public Enemy Number One':

A

---

1 Briefly describe the appearance of the people in the queue.
2 Suggest why a gangster and 'Public Enemy', Al Capone, provided free soup for the unemployed in Chicago.
3 What light does the fact that Capone opened this soup kitchen throw on US society at that time?

What was it like to be on the breadline? Karl Monroe, an out-of-work newspaper reporter, described his experience of the breadline in a magazine article in 1930:

B Tired, hungry, and cold, I stretched out on the bench, and despite the lack of downy mattress and comforter* eventually fell asleep. The soles of my feet were swollen with blisters, because my shoes had not been removed in at least seventy-two hours and I had tramped the sidewalks for three days. . . .

    * quilt

    Finally, I stood in the breadline in Twenty-Fifth Street, where the women's section of the Socialist Party daily distributed soup, coffee and bread. To my surprise, I found in the line all types of men – the majority being skilled craftsmen unable to find work. One of them told me he had been a civil engineer and had earned $8,000 a year. Since losing his job almost a year ago, he had drifted from bad to worse, occasionally picking up odd jobs, until he had sunk to the breadline. . . .

    There are many men who still hope despite months of failure. Of a dozen men in the park of nights, at least eight will tell you they have something in mind for the following day, and they actually convince themselves. A few nights later a casual search will reveal the same men, still with 'something in mind for tomorrow'. . . . In the meantime, they read, under the arc light in the park, in second-hand newspapers, predictions that business will be normal again in sixty days.

From Susan Winslow, Brother Can You Spare a Dime?, Paddington Press, 1976.

---

1 In source B, why do you think Karl Monroe had 'tramped the sidewalks for three days' before joining the breadline?
2 Suggest why he was surprised to find 'all kinds of men in the breadline'?

Many of the people who lost their jobs also lost their homes. Those who could not afford to pay rent or to keep up their mortgage repayments often had to live rough. Another journalist, Charles Walker, wrote about the plight of such people in 1932:

C A few weeks ago I visited the incinerator and public dump at Youngstown, Ohio. Back of the garbage house there are at least three acres of waste land, humpy with ash heaps and junk. . . . The place is . . . a shanty town, or rather a collection of shanty hamlets. Many of them are caves with tin roofs, but all of them blend with the place, for they are constructed out of it. From 150 to 200 men live in the shanties. The place is called by its inhabitants – Hooverville*.

I went forward and talked to the men; they showed me their houses. These vary greatly from mere caves covered with a piece of tin, to weather-proof shanties built of packing boxes and equipped with a stolen window-frame or an improvised door. Some have beds and one or two a kitchen stove rescued from the junk heap, though most of the men cook in communal fashion over a fire shielded by bricks in the open.

The inhabitants were not, as one might expect, outcasts or 'untouchables', or even hoboes* in the American sense; they were men without jobs. Life is sustained by begging, eating at the city soup kitchens, or earning a quarter by polishing an automobile – enough to bring home bacon and bread. Eating 'at home' is preferred. The location of the town also has its commissary* advantage; men take part of their food from the garbage house. This I entered; the stench of decaying food is appalling. Here I found that there were more women than men – gathering food for their families. In Hooverville there were no women.

*after President Hoover, 1929–33

* tramps

* food supply

From Charles R. Walker, *Relief and Revolution*, The Forum LXXXVIII, 1932.

---

1 Judging by sources A, B and C, what kinds of men were most likely to end up on breadlines and in Hoovervilles?
2 Suggest why there were no women in the Hooverville in source C.
3 Bearing in mind that sources A, B and C are the work of professional newspaper journalists,
  (a) why do you think they found the subject of hunger and homelessness newsworthy?
  (b) do you have any reason to doubt the reliability of the sources as historical evidence?

The figure of fifteen million Americans out of work by 1933 does not reflect the total number of people who suffered as a result of mass unemployment. The families of unemployed workers also suffered: so did the families of workers reduced to part-time work. In all, between thirty and forty million Americans had an inadequate income by 1933, and the inevitable result was hunger. This letter to a local newspaper in 1933 illustrates the hardship in which one family was living:

D Living on $1.50 a week
Our slip* called for two dollars a week [and those in charge of relief] thought any woman could prepare forty-two meals a week on a dollar-fifty for two people. So we got fifty cents taken from the two dollars.

Those in charge of relief have never known actual hunger and want, have never lain awake at night worrying about unpaid rent, or how to make a few groceries do for the seemingly endless seven days till the next week's order of groceries. . . . It gives me the nightmare, but I'm used to it.

* an order for food that could be obtained from the town food depot

But we are supposed to have faith in our government. We are told to keep cheerful and smiling. Just what does our government expect us to do when our rent is due? When we need a doctor? When we need clothes? We haven't had a tube of toothpaste in weeks and have to check off some item of needed food when we get soap. I can only do my washing every two weeks, because that is as often as I can get oil for the oil stove to heat wash water and laundry soap to do my washing.

It is always the people with full stomachs who tell us poor people to keep happy. I should love to have some new clothes, and I should enjoy a radio the same as anybody. But try to get them!

No work, no hope; just live one day to the next. Maybe better times are coming. Personally, I doubt it.

                                    A Small Town Housewife.

Quoted in Robert S. Lynd and Helen Merrell Lynd, *Middletown in Transition: A Study in Cultural Conflicts,* Constable and Co., 1937.

---

1 Why, according to source D, was $1.50 a week not enough to provide for a family? Why do you think those in charge of relief payments thought that it was?

2 What do you think this woman hoped to achieve by writing this letter to her local newspaper?

Another letter written in 1934 shows that the 'Small Town Housewife' in source D was right to doubt that better times were coming. It is one of fifteen million letters written by ordinary Americans in the 1930s and sent to the White House, home of the US President.

E

                                    Aug. 6, 1934
                                    Newcomb, Tenn.

Mr J. Will Taylor*,

I am enclosing you a few lines for instructions if you pleas I am here with 5 five children and a wife and . . . I cant get a days work at eny thing at all I havt had a days work for over two 2 years I am a disable body man and cant get a days work at all. I am a ruptured man my family is barfooted and naked and an suferns and we all are a goin to purish if I cannot get some help some way I cant get any ade at all and if I could get it in Scot County where it is from me I could not get it for it is about 20 miles to the clostly rail rode station from where I live in the county. I have got no horse no autmobel and no nothing to ride can you pleas if posible fix for me to get some help some way can you fix for me some way so my family will not purish.

So hoping to here from you soon from

                                    NP

* The Congressman for Tennessee

From Robert S. McElvaine (ed.), *Down and Out in the Depression,* University of North Carolina Press, 1983.

---

1 Why, according to source E, could the writer of the letter get neither work nor relief?

2 How useful as evidence of people's suffering in the Great Depression do you think letters like sources D and E are? Explain your answer.

There are millions more letters, memoirs and articles written during the Depression years which paint a picture of hardship and suffering. Equally, there are many sources which suggest that the Depression was not as bad as it might seem. For example, Henry Ford, the motor-car manufacturer, said in March 1931, when eight million Americans were out of work:

F The average man won't really do a day's work unless he is caught and cannot get out of it. There is plenty of work to do, if people would do it.

Quoted in Susan Winslow, *Brother Can You Spare A Dime?*, Paddington Press, 1976.

A newspaper editorial at the start of the Depression in 1929 made a similar point:

G This is a free country of boundless opportunity which guarantees an equal chance to everybody. If people don't get ahead it isn't the fault of society.

Unfortunately there has always been in this and every other society a fringe of 'unfortunates'. Things like this just happen.

But these things 'happen' usually in part at least because the people involved have violated the gospel of 'hard work and thrift'.

Therefore society should not do too much for them because such extra help 'weakens the character' of the recipient.

Quoted in Robert S. Lynd and Helen Merrell Lynd, *Middletown in Transition: A Study in Cultural Conflicts*, Constable and Co., 1937.

---

1 In your own words, briefly summarise the arguments in sources F and G.
2 To what extent are the arguments in sources F and G supported by sources A to E in this chapter? Explain your answer.

And years later, a resident of Manhattan, one of New York's wealthiest districts, said this in an interview:

H I don't think we ever mentioned the people on relief. Friends did in private at the breakfast table or at cocktail time. But never socially. Because I always had a theory – when you're out with friends, out socially, everything must be charming, and you don't allow the ugly.

There were no apple sellers – not in New York. Never, never. There were a few beggars. One day, I saw this pathetic beggar, whom I'd always felt sorry for. This Cadillac drove up. I'd just given him a quarter* and it picked him up. There was a woman driving it. And I thought: well, if they can drive a Cadillac, they don't need my quarter.

I never saw one breadline, never in New York. If they were they were in Harlem or down in Greenwich Village. They were never in this section of town. The 'New Deal' meant absolutely nothing to me except higher taxation. The thirties was a glamorous, glittering moment.

* *25 cent coin*

From Studs Terkel, *Hard Times: An Oral History of the Great Depression*, Allen Lane, 1970.

1 Assuming for the moment that the speaker was telling the truth, why do you think he never saw a breadline in New York?

2 Do you have any reason to doubt the truthfulness of the speaker? Explain your answer.

In the Presidential election campaign of 1932, the Democratic Party candidate, Franklin Delano Roosevelt, offered voters a 'New Deal' if they elected him President. He called for 'the building of plans that put their faith once more in the forgotten man at the bottom of the economic pyramid'. President Herbert Hoover, the Republican Party's candidate, warned of terrible dangers ahead if the voters put Roosevelt into the White House. In a speech in October 1932, shortly before the election, he said:

This campaign is more than a contest between two men. It is more than a contest between parties. It is a contest between two philosophies of government.

We are told by the opposition that we must have a change, that we must have a new deal. It is not the change . . . to which I object, but the proposal to alter the whole foundations of our national life. . . . They are proposing changes and so-called new deals which would destroy the very foundations of our American system. . . .

Our system is the product of our race and of our experience in building a nation unparalleled in the whole history of the world. It is a system peculiar to the American people. It differs essentially from all others in the world. It is an American system.

It is founded on the conception that only through ordered liberty, through freedom to the individual, and equal opportunity to the individual will his initiative and enterprise be summoned to spur the march of progress. . . .

This whole American system is . . . founded upon the conception of responsibility of the individual to the community, of the responsibility of local government to the state, of the state to the national government. . . .

These [new deal] measures would transfer vast responsibilities to the Federal Government from the states, the local governments and the individuals. . .; they would break down our form of government.

From William Starr Myers and Walter H. Newton, *The Hoover Administration: A Documented Narrative*, Charles Scribner's Sons, 1936.

1 In your own words, briefly summarise Hoover's objections to Roosevelt's New Deal.

2 To whom do you think Hoover's views might have appealed?

Roosevelt won the Presidential election of 1932 and put his 'New Deal' plans into effect within weeks of taking office in 1933. Using the full powers of the federal government, Roosevelt and his Cabinet set up federal agencies to provide work for the unemployed. The Civilian

Conservation Corps, the Tennessee Valley Authority, the Public Works Administration and the National Recovery Administration were just some of the 'alphabet agencies' created in 1933. American opinion was immediately and bitterly divided by the New Deal, with millions of people loathing every aspect of it. Thomas Wolfe, an American writer, described what happened when he said at a dinner table that he intended to vote for Roosevelt:

J . . . boiled shirts began to roll up their backs like window-shades. Maidenly necks which a moment before were as white and graceful as the swan's became instantly so distended with the energies of patriotic rage that diamond dog-collars and ropes of pearls were snapped and sent flying like so many pieces of string. I was told that if I voted for this vile Communist, this sinister fascist, this scheming and contriving socialist and his gang of conspirators, I had no longer any right to consider myself an American citizen.

From Elizabeth Nowell (ed.), *The Letters of Thomas Wolfe*, Charles Scribner's Sons, 1956.

1 In what ways does Thomas Wolfe exaggerate in source J?
2 Does the fact that he exaggerates affect the value of source J as evidence of anti-New Deal opinion?

A letter sent to Roosevelt's wife Eleanor spelled out what some people thought of the New Deal's effects on their town:

K   Dec 14–1937
                              Columbus, Ind.
Mrs F. D. Roosevelt
Washington, D.C.
Mrs Roosevelt,
   I suppose from your point of view the work relief, old age pensions, slum clearance and all the rest seems like a perfect remedy for all the ills of this country, but I would like for you to see the results, as the other half see them.
   We have always had a shiftless, never-do-well class of people whose one and only aim in life is to live without work. . . .
   There has never been any necessity for any one who is able to work, being on relief in this locality, but there have been many eating the bread of charity and they have lived better than ever before. I have had taxpayers tell me that their children come home from school and asked why they couldn't have nice lunches like the children on relief. . . .
                              M. A. H.

From Robert S. McElvaine (ed.), *Down and Out in the Depression*, University of North Carolina Press, 1983.

1 What further objections to the New Deal are revealed by sources J and K?
2 Write a reply to the letter in source K as if you were Eleanor Roosevelt.

The criticisms and complaints about the New Deal were endless. Roosevelt himself was attacked as a Communist, a Fascist, a Socialist, a madman, a simpleton, and a thousand other names. But, as one wit remarked, 'Everyone was against the New Deal but the voters'. The 1936 Presidential election gave Roosevelt the greatest electoral victory in US history up to then, as well as Democratic majorities in both houses of Congress. His re-election in both 1940 and 1944 meant that, alone among the American Presidents, he was elected President on four successive occasions.

Using the sources in this chapter as evidence:
1 List the ways in which ordinary Americans were affected by the Great Depression.
2 Explain why many Americans did not want the federal government to help those who were out of work, homeless or hungry.
3 Suggest why the issues of unemployment and poverty aroused such strong feelings.

7 The organisation of terror: Hitler's Germany, 1933–45

As the Allied armies rolled across defeated Germany early in 1945 they took possession of a number of prison camps known to their inmates and guards as KZ camps – *Konzentrationlager*, or 'concentration camps'. General Eisenhower, Supreme Commander of the Allied forces, visited a KZ camp at Buchenwald in southern Germany. 'The things I saw,' he wrote in a letter shortly afterwards, 'beggar description. The visual evidence and the verbal testimony of starvation, cruelty and bestiality were so overpowering as to leave me a bit sick.'

The idea of concentrating large numbers of prisoners behind barbed wire fences was not a German invention. The British had used concentration camps in the Boer War, as had a number of countries in the First World War. But what Eisenhower and the Allied forces saw at Buchenwald in 1945 had no comparison with the camps of those earlier wars. Piles of naked corpses, cages filled with scarecrow men dying from starvation, instruments of torture, execution and medical experiment, all showed that the Nazis had abandoned every standard of law and humanity in dealing with their prisoners.

'I made the visit,' Eisenhower went on, 'in order to be able to give *first-hand* evidence of these things if ever, in the future, there develops a tendency to charge these allegations merely to "propaganda".' Eisenhower also arranged for photographers, for journalists, for politicians, and for civilians living near Buchenwald to view the terrible scenes in the camp. And as the other camps were liberated in 1945 a horrified public began to realise what Nazi rule had meant for some ten million human beings who had been taken into the camps.

The first of the Nazi concentration camps was set up at Dachau, near Munich in southern Germany, on 9 March 1933. The camp, a group of huts in a disused gravel-pit, held around 5,000 critics of the new Nazi government, and was run by the local Dachau SS, already notorious for their brutality. The nature and purpose of the camp can be seen in source A, an extract from the camp's 'Regulations for Discipline and Punishment' published on 1 October 1933:

A Tolerance means weakness.... Punishment will be mercilessly handed out whenever the interests of the fatherland warrant it.... No. 6 The following are punishable with eight days' solitary confinement, and twenty-five strokes to be administered before and after the serving of the sentence:
1. Anyone making derogatory or ironical remarks to a member of the SS, deliberately omitting the prescribed marks of respect, or in any other way demonstrating unwillingness to submit himself to disciplinary measures ...
No. 11 In accordance with the law on revolutionaries, the following offenders, considered as agitators, will be hanged. Anyone who ... discusses politics, carries on controversial talks and meetings, forms cliques, loiters around with others: who, for the purpose of supplying the propaganda of the opposition with atrocity stories, collects true or false information about the concentration camp; receives such information, buries it, talks about it to others, smuggles

it out of the camp into the hands of foreign visitors or others. . . .
No. 12 Anyone who physically attacks a guard or SS man. . .will be
shot on the spot as a mutineer or subsequently hanged. . . .
No. 19 Confinement will be in a cell, with a hard bed, and with
bread and water. The prisoner will receive warm food every four
days. Punitive work consists of severe physical or particularly dirty
work, performed under close supervision. Incidental punishments
are: drillings, beatings, withholding of mail and food, hard rest, tying
to stakes, reprimands and warnings. . . .

Service Regulations for Prisoner Escorts and Guards
Anyone letting a prisoner escape will be arrested and handed over
to the Bavarian Political Police for liberating prisoners through
negligence.

If a prisoner attempts to escape, he is to be shot without warning.
The guard who has shot an escaping prisoner in the line of duty
will not be punished.

If a prisoner attacks a guard, the latter is to resist the attack not
by physical force but by the use of his weapons. A guard dis-
regarding this regulation must expect immediate dismissal. In any
case anyone who keeps his back covered will seldom have to worry
about an attack.

If a unit of prisoners mutinies or revolts, it is to be shot at by
all supervising guards. Warning shots are forbidden on
principle. . . .

From *Nuremburg Trial Document,
778-P5*, 1945.

---

1 List ten punishments laid down in these regulations.
2 Are any of the regulations and punishments, in your opinion, inhumane? Explain your answer.
3 How might the 'Service Regulations for Prisoner Escorts and Guards' have affected the behaviour of young or newly-recruited guards? Explain your answer.
4 In your opinion, can source A be reliably used as evidence of Nazi attitudes towards discipline and punishment? Explain your answer.

The Dachau Regulations were extended to all concentration camps in September 1934. Life in the camps under those regulations can be glimpsed in source B, a statement made by an anonymous Jewish prisoner to a charity organisation working in Germany in 1938. It was published by the British government in 1939, at the start of the Second World War, in a pamphlet called 'Papers concerning the Treatment of German Nationals in Germany, 1938–39'.

B Timetable: 3.30 a.m., get up (bed about 10 p.m.), very bad air; smell
appalling; water drips down the tiny cellar windows. Form ranks at
4.30. Coffee distribution at 4.45 on the square where the gallows
stand and the blocks (for flogging). . . . 5.30 a.m., end of roll call;
until then stand stiffly to attention. Those who have reported sick
now come forward, are separated off and inspected by the Comman-

dant. He at once treats the 'fit' with his riding whip, in the face, in the presence of others; "Jews do not fall ill." The Commandant decides by sight who is 'ripe' for the doctor. These number 6 or 7 per cent; the others have to go back into the labour gang. No differentiation of the sick in the labour gang; they are helped on by kicks and riding whip. . . . The work consists of stone-breaking a quarter of an hour away from the road which is to be built. It is outside the camp but within the charged wires. Attempts at flight occur, but all end with shooting. Many end their sufferings by feigning flight in order to be shot down. Everywhere sentries are posted around. A colony of 'cripples', men with wooden legs, ruptures (sometimes if their belts are lost the ruptures break out again), are obliged to carry massive stones at the will of the guard. They included old men of 70 who are utterly unequal to the work. . . . At 11.30 comes the midday pause (although sometimes work is enforced till 7 o'clock without food.) 12.30, work resumed till 3.30. 4 p.m., roll-call. This generally lasts till 5.30; for many of the 'Jew people' till 10. How 'Non-Aryans' are distinguished from Jews is not clear. Woe to the non-Aryan who by mistake gets among the Aryans. Jews have to wear the 'David Cross' with the sign: red for 'professional criminal', black for the 'work shy', lilac for the 'Bible bug'. One is compelled to sign oneself as a 'professional criminal', and it goes on the card index. (On the other side of the card one's real profession is stated.) Woe to him who refuses to sign the statement! Yellow is the sign for a Jew and has to be added to the other.

The floggings take place at the afternoon roll-call, the individuals having to step forward. The penalties are read out (being fixed beforehand). Normal punishment is twenty-five strokes on the seat, carried out by two guards standing on each side with riding whips. The prisoner is lashed to a board. If he cries out the strokes are increased up to thirty-five. The guards use all their force, sometimes springing into the air so as to bring the arm down with increased momentum. Few days pass without cases of flogging, and the number may be from two to ten. . . .

From *Papers Concerning the Treatment of German Nationals in Germany 1938–1939*, His Majesty's Stationery Office, 1939.

---

1 What kinds of people were imprisoned in Buchenwald concentration camp, according to source B?
2 How do sources A and B suggest that the general public was unlikely to find out about conditions in concentration camps?
3 Does the fact that source B is (a) anonymous, and (b) reported at second-hand by an unnamed charity organisation, affect its value as historical evidence? Explain your answer.
4 Why do you think the British government published source B in 1939? Does this affect its value as historical evidence?

Despite the difficulty of getting information about concentration camps, enough rumours and stories about them circulated for people to know something of their methods. This is reflected in a broadcast on

German radio by Heinrich Himmler, the head of the SS and Chief of German Police, on 21 September 1939:

C I know how mendaciously and foolishly people abroad write and tell tales about and run down this institution. Concentration camp is certainly, like any form of deprivation of liberty, a tough and strict measure. Hard productive labour, a regular life, exceptional cleanliness in matters of daily life and personal hygiene, splendid food, strict but fair treatment, instruction in how to work again and how to learn the necessary crafts – these are the methods of education. The motto which stands above these camps reads: there is a path to freedom. Its milestones are: obedience, hard work, orderliness, cleanliness, sobriety, truthfulness, self-sacrifice and love of the fatherland.

Quoted in J. Noakes and G. Pridham (eds.), *Nazism 1919–1945*, vol. 2, *State, Economy and Society, 1933–39*, University of Exeter, 1984.

---

1 How does source B contradict Himmler's claims in source C?
2 Which parts of the German population do you think Himmler was hoping to convince with this broadcast?

In the five years after that, the organisation of terror had become so refined that by 1944 even children had their own concentration camp. Source G, a report by a German judge dated 31 July 1944, describes how youngsters were organised in the Moringen youth concentration camp near Gottingen:

D Pupils who are difficult, deviant in character, suffering from emotional inadequacies, hyperactive, excitable, discontented in disposition, bad-tempered, incorrigable mischief-makers or determined petty criminals . . . are clear custody cases. In line with the practice of the Institute of Criminal Biology and of this camp, these pupils are termed 'trouble-makers' and, as soon as they are identified as such, assigned to S Block [Trouble Makers' Block] . . .

Pupils with personality weaknesses, who are unsettled and lacking in drive, who cannot pass any of the proficiency tests and have an unfailing tendency to aberrancy, are also custody cases without exception. They are allotted to D Block [Persistent Failures Block] . . .

Those who are primarily unstable, irresponsible or lacking in independence, who are severely at risk and liable to recidivism, go into G Block [Occasional Failures Block].

Quoted in Detlev J. K. Peukert, *Inside Nazi Germany: Conformity, Opposition and Racism in Everyday Life*, (translated by Richard Deveson), Batsford, 1987.

The greatest expansion in the concentration camp network took place after the Nazi conquest of Europe in 1940–41 when the Nazi leaders decided upon a 'final solution of the Jewish question' in the areas under their control. This meant the killing of all Jews, either by working them to death or by clinical murder. To deal with the estimated eleven million Jews living in Europe, five 'extermination camps' were built in remote areas of German-occupied Poland, at Belzec, Treblinka, Sobibor, Chelmno and Auschwitz-Birkenau. Each camp was linked to the rest of 'Greater Germany' by rail, and to transport captured Jews to the camps long trains of cattle trucks ran according to strict timetables. One such train was described by a Polish railway worker, Franciszek Zabecki, in a book of memoirs published in 1977:

E The train was made up of sixty covered wagons, crammed with people. There were old people, young people, men, women, children and infants in quilts. The doors of the wagons were bolted, the air gaps had a grating of barbed wire. Several SS men, with automatic weapons ready to shoot, stood on the foot-boards of the wagons on both sides of the trains and even lay on the roofs.

It was a hot day; people in the wagons were fainting. The SS guards with rolled up sleeves looked like butchers. . . .

After the transport arrived, some fiendish spirit got into the SS men; they drew their pistols, put them away, and took them out again, as if they wanted to shoot and kill straight away; they approached the wagons, silencing those who were shrieking and wailing, and again they swore and screamed.

Shouting '*Tempo, schnell*,' 'At the double, quickly,' to the German railwaymen who had come from Sokolow Podlaski, they went off to the camp, to take over their victims there 'properly'. On the wagons we could see chalk marks giving the number of people in the wagon, viz.: 120, 150, 180 and 200 people. We worked out later that the total number of people in the train must have been about eight to ten thousand.

The 'settlers' were strangely huddled together in the wagons. All of them had to stand, without sufficient air and without access to toilet facilities. It was like travelling in hot ovens. The high temperature, lack of air, and the hot weather created conditions that not even healthy, young, strong organisms could stand. Moans, shouts, weeping, calls for water or for a doctor issued from the wagons. And protests: 'How can people be treated so inhumanly?' 'When will they let us leave the wagons altogether?'

Through some air gaps terrified people looked out, asking hopefully: 'How far is it to the agricultural estates where we're going to work?'

From Franciszek Zabecki, *Old and New Memories of the Tragedy of the Jews at Treblinka, Warsaw, 1977.*

---

1 Judging by source E, what had the Polish railway workers and the passengers been told about the destination and purpose of the train?
2 Why did the writer of source E suspect that the destination and purpose of the train were different from what he had been told?

Once a train had arrived at a death camp, passengers were divided into those who were to work and those who were to die immediately. The fate of those selected for work can be seen in this drawing done by one of them, a teenage girl named Ella Lieberman. It was found by Allied soldiers in the Auschwitz-Birkenau camp at the end of the war.

F   Source: Museum of Auschwitz.

1 Using the drawing as evidence, describe the conditions of life of prisoners in Auschwitz-Birkenau camp.
2 Bearing in mind that Regulation 11 of concentration camp rules (source A, page 46) forbade the collection of information about camps, on pain of death, why do you think Ella Lieberman did this drawing?
3 How reliable and how useful do you consider the drawing as evidence of conditions in the extermination camps? Explain your answer.

Kurt Gerstein, an SS officer captured and interrogated by the Allies in 1945, described what happened to those selected to die in Belzec extermination camp in 1942:

G A little before seven, there was an announcement: 'The first train will arrive in ten minutes!' A few minutes later a train arrives from Lemberg: forty-five cars arrive with more than six thousand people; two hundred Ukrainians assigned to this work flung open the doors and drove the Jews out of the cars with leather whips.

A loudspeaker gave instructions: 'Strip, even artificial limbs and glasses. Hand all money and valuables in at the 'valuables' window. Women and young girls are to have their hair cut in the "barber's hut".'. . .

Then the march began. Barbed wire on both sides, in the rear two dozen Ukrainians with rifles. They drew near. Wirth and I found ourselves in front of the death chambers. Stark naked men, women, children and cripples passed by. A tall SS man in the corner called to the unfortunates in a loud minister's voice: "Nothing is going to hurt you! Just breathe deep and it will strengthen your lungs. It's a way to prevent contagious diseases. It's a good disinfectant!"

They asked him what was going to happen and he answered: "The men will have to work, build houses and streets. The women won't have to do that. They will be busy with the housework and the kitchen."

This was the last hope for some of these poor people, enough to make them march toward the death chambers without resistance. The majority knew everything; the smell betrayed it!. . .

SS men pushed the men into the chambers. "Fill it up," Wirth ordered. Seven to eight hundred people in ninety-three square metres. . . .

Heckenholt tried to start the motor. It wouldn't start! Captain Wirth came up. You could see he was afraid because I was there to see the disaster. Yes, I saw everything and waited. My stopwatch clocked it all: fifty minutes. Seventy minutes and the diesel still would not start. . . .

Captain Wirth, furious, struck with his whip the Ukrainian who helped Heckenholt. The diesel engine started up after two hours and forty-nine minutes by my stopwatch. Twenty-five minutes passed. You could see through the window that many were already dead, for an electric light illuminated the interior of the room. All were dead after thirty-two minutes.

Jewish workers on the other side opened the wooden doors. They had been promised their lives in return for doing this horrible work, plus a small percentage of the money and valuables collected. The people were still standing like columns of stone, with no room to fall or lean. Even in death you could tell the families, all holding hands. It was difficult to separate them while emptying out the room for the next batch. The bodies were tossed out. . . . Two dozen workers were busy checking mouths which they opened with iron hooks. . . . Dentists knocked out gold teeth, bridges and crowns with hammers.

Captain Wirth stood in the middle of them. He was in his element and, showing me a big jam box filled with teeth, said, 'See the weight of the gold! Just from yesterday and the day before! You can't imagine what we find every day, dollars, diamonds, gold! . . .'

From *Nuremburg Trial Document P5-2170*, 1945.

1 Why do you think the guards kept lying to the Jewish prisoners about what was going to happen to them, right up to the moment when they were locked in the gas chamber?
2 Suggest why the author of source G timed the events he witnessed with a stopwatch.
3 Bearing in mind that source G is a statement made under interrogation at the end of the war, how reliable do you consider it as evidence about Nazi extermination camps? Explain your answer.

Between 1939 and 1945 the German Nazis and their collaborators killed some six million Jews. They also murdered more than ten million Gypsies, Russian prisoners-of-war, homosexuals, 'mental defectives', Slavs, and anyone else who had no place in their 'New Order'. In the camps, where the majority of these murders took place, Nazis also carried out torture and medical experiments on their victims. And, as the sources in this chapter suggest, lies, deceptions and censorship were used to cover up this crime against humanity. However, the end of the war came too quickly for the Nazis to conceal all traces of the crime, and the advancing Allied armies revealed the full horror of it as they liberated the camps. Source H, from the front page of a British newspaper dated 19 April 1945, shows what they found in two of the camps – Belsen and Buchenwald.

H

Source: *News Chronicle.*

Belsen camp: The full, terrible story

From COLIN WILLS
News Chronicle War Correspondent

In Belsen Prison Camp, Tuesday (delayed).

I SPENT yesterday, last night and today here. The worst horrors I described in yesterday's dispatch are far exceeded by what I have seen since.

I got here immediately after the place had been overrun by the British 11th Armoured Division. Only a small detachment of British troops had then arrived, and it was awaiting reinforcements to take over the administration of this vast area and its 60,000 inhabitants from hundreds of Hungarian guards, with a considerable force of the Wehrmacht and between 50 and 100 S.S. men.

When I returned from sending yesterday's dispatch there were more dead lying where they had fallen from starvation.

MORE WERE DYING

Other prisoners, feeble though they were, were lifting the dead into blankets and carrying them away.

The bodies were terribly light, yet the carrying of them taxed the strength of the others.

Dozens more were lying on earth banks against walls, obviously dying. British medical units were driving up scarred roads through smoking villages where the battle had just passed and pockets of the enemy still held out in the woods, and they had not yet got here.

Neither had a food convoy nor a water convoy—perhaps more important still.

In the meantime soldiers had given out what water and tea they could.

One man, unable to stand up, sprawled on his belly across a pile of rubbish, cup to lips. He looked like a yellow stick wrapped in grey rag.

A man who had been there only one week told me he had nothing whatever to eat on three or four days, he could not remember which.

On the other days he had ¼ litre (nearly ½ pint) of turnip soup, and one day a thin slice of bread with a teaspoonful of sour milk cheese. "I am weak already after a week," he said, "and my legs and arms are shrunken, for we have had to work on that diet."

"How about those who have been here many months?"

"Well, look around. Can you see a blade of grass? You won't find one. They have eaten all the grass."

Hanging rag

An elderly Jew was shuffling slowly from one group of soldiers

MONTY MOVING ON

Here, and in pictures on the back page today, the eyes of British men and women may behold for the first time some of the more revolting features of Nazi guilt. These are official pictures and the News Chronicle has decided to print them, because it is right that the world should see at close quarters indisputable proof of Ger-

INDISPUTABLE PROOF
By the Editor

many's crimes against the human race.

Other pictures, still more horrible in detail than these, have been circulated by the military authorities, but the selection here published tell their own story plainly enough. Many times reports of Nazi cruelty and torture have seemed almost too monstrous to be true; but here is evidence that none can question and it is proper that decent citizens should look it in the face.

It is welcome news that the Allied commanders on the spot are compelling the neighbouring German population to visit the scenes of this abomination and carry out the task of burying the dead and tending the human wreckage that still survives. Every German in the Reich should be forced to see the handiwork of his fellow-countrymen: careful records should be kept, films made and exhibitions arranged at which attendance should be compulsory.

MAKING THEM SEE THE EVIDENCE
German men and women from Weimar are made to stand in a yard at Buchenwald concentration camp. In front of them is a lorry, piled high with the bodies of prisoners, which was found at the camp

Poland: three Powers to confer in U.S.

CAPTURED GENER TEN A PENNY

1 Why do you think the German men and women from Weimar, shown in the newspaper photograph, were made to visit Buchenwald concentration camp?
2 Can photographs like the one in source H be considered 'indisputable proof of Germany's crimes against the human race'?

---

1 Why do you think that General Eisenhower thought in 1945 that there might in the future be a tendency 'to charge these allegations merely to propaganda'?
2 Suggest why concentration camps were headline news in 1945 (source H) but not in 1939, even though the bad conditions in them were already public knowledge at that time (see source B).
3 Using sources A to H as evidence, give as many reasons as you can to explain why there was so much cruelty and brutality in the concentration camps.
4 (a) In your opinion, how likely was it that people living close to concentration camps in the 1930s and 1940s knew what was happening inside them?
  (b) What actions might such people have taken after finding out what was happening inside the camps?

8 The Great Purge: Stalin and the Soviet Union, 1935–38

Between 1935 and 1938 around seven million Soviet citizens were arrested by tthe NKVD – the Peoples' Commissariat of Internal Affairs, or secret police. Of these, probably three million died in the labour camps run by the NKVD, either from deliberate ill-treatment or by execution. What was the purpose of this mass terror?

The official explanation was that a vast conspiracy had affected every part of society. The aim of this alleged conspiracy, which was organised by disgraced Communist Party leaders such as Trotsky, Kamenev and Zinoviev, was to overthrow the government, sabotage industry and food supplies, defeat the USSR in war, and restore capitalism. Those arrested were all involved in the conspiracy, it was claimed.

To the ordinary citizen, however, the arrests seemed to involve everybody and anybody. Apart from the disgraced Party leaders, whose 'crimes' were exposed in well-publicised show trials, there was usually no obvious reason why people were arrested. Often the charges defied belief: honest and long-serving members of the Party were arrested as Fascist agents; Chinese people were arrested as Japanese spies, Jews as agents of the Nazi Gestapo. Railway engine drivers were shot as 'wreckers' for driving their locomotives too fast and as 'limiters' for driving them too slow.

The sources in this chapter have been chosen to show how and why the Great Purge of 1935–38 began, and how it spread to involve so many people.

The Great Purge began shortly after the assassination of Sergei Kirov, Secretary of the Leningrad Party organisation, on 1 December 1934. That same evening, Stalin issued the following decree:

A 1. Investigative agencies are directed to speed up the cases of those accused of the preparation or execution of acts of terror;

2. Judicial organs are directed not to hold up the execution of death sentences pertaining to crimes of this category in order to consider the possibility of pardon. . . .

3. The organs of the Commissariat of Internal Affairs are directed to execute the death sentences against criminals of the above-mentioned category immediately after the passage of sentences.

From Nikita Khrushchev, *Confidential Report to the 20th Party Congress*, 1956.

---

1 What was the Commissariat of Internal Affairs? What is unusual about giving an organisation like this the power to carry out death sentences?

2 How did this decree make it likely that people would be arrested and executed for crimes they had not committed?

Several weeks after the murder of Kirov, the Central Committee of the Communist Party sent a letter to all local Party organisations throughout the USSR. It was entitled 'Lessons of the Events bound up with the Evil Murder of Comrade Kirov'. The letter urged all local Party organisations to hold meetings in order to investigate their members and to expel 'alien elements'. The identity of 'alien elements' was to be established by inviting members to denounce fellow members whom they suspected.

In Smolensk, a typical Soviet city 400 km west of Moscow, 4,100 Party members underwent investigation. Of these, 455 were purged, or expelled, from the Party. Their expulsion was based on the evidence of 712 oral denunciations made in public at Party meetings, and 200 written denunciations. The reasons for their expulsion are listed in source B, one of many thousands of Party documents captured by the Germans when they invaded the USSR in 1941:

B *On the results of the Investigation of Party Documents of the Members of the Smolensk City and Raion* Party Organisation*   * district

1. Agents of the enemy (spies and those connected with them)   7
2. White Guardists and participants in counter-revolutionary uprisings   12
3. Remnants of counter-revolutionary, anti-Party groupings of Trotskyites and Zinovievites   11
4. Those who left other parties, changing only on the surface   9
5. Swindlers who used the Party apparatus to obtain Party documents   2
6. Swindlers who procured Party cards by deceitful means   5
7. Those from a class-alien and hostile background who concealed their past   99
8. People who do not inspire trust and who betray the interests of the Party   127
9. People who have a criminal past (13 of them embezzlers) 53
10. Deserters from the Red Army   12
11. Those accepted in violation of the Party rules   9
12. Those who evaded the purge of the Party in 1929 and 1933   3
13. Those who evaded the investigation of Party documents   3
14. Those corrupt in a moral and ethical sense   32
15. Those who take an anti-Party attitude towards Party documents   38
16. Those who were alienated from the Party and who violated the rules of the Party on the payment of their membership dues, etc.   33

Quoted in Merle Fainsod, *Smolensk Under Soviet Rule*, Macmillan, 1959.

---

1 What were the two most common reasons for expulsion from the Smolensk Party organisation?
2 Suggest what such people might have done to merit expulsion from the Party.

An example of the 200 written denunciations which led to the purge in Smolensk can be seen in source C. It is a letter from the Smolensk Party files, and, like source B, was seized by the German army during the invasion of the USSR in 1941:

C To the Western Oblast* Committee of the CPSU(b)†

Secret

* Region

† Communist Party of the Soviet Union

After reading the ... letter of the Central Committee of the CPSU(b) ... I called to mind Trotskyites who actively struggled against the Party. I remember that in 1925–26 ... there worked in the Volost* committee at that time an agitator and propagandist named Karkuzevich, whose first name was apparently Michael, a member of the CPSU(b) since 1917, and a railway worker. Karkuzevich at that time was an active Trotskyite. He not only slandered the Party and its leader, Comrade Stalin, but things went so far that he clearly refused to carry out the decisions of the Fourteenth Party Congress in the Party network, since he did not agree with these decisions and considered them incorrect.... I am offering this information so that the necessary steps can be taken.

* Township

Quoted in Merle Fainsod, *Smolensk Under Soviet Rule*, Macmillan, 1959.

---

1 Judging by this letter, what had Michael Karkuzevich done wrong?
2 What do you think was the motive of the writer in sending this letter?
3 Into which of the categories in source B do you think Michael Karkuzevich was placed?

The fate of people who were purged from the Party can be seen in this letter written by a Party official in Smolensk in October 1935. Like sources B and C, it comes from the mass of documents captured by the Germans in 1941:

D In connection with the check of Party documents, many complaints reach us in the Obkom* from those expelled from the Party to the effect that after their expulsion from the Party they are dismissed from work and are in general not allowed to do any kind of work. Dismissal from work, without grounds, in connection with expulsion from the Party, is incorrect. ... I wish to make clear that only those expelled from the Party who are clearly unmasked enemies and socially dangerous elements should be dismissed from work. It is necessary, where possible to isolate such people, to arrest or banish them. ... Persons ... should not be dismissed from work if they do not seem socially dangerous. It is understood that it is necessary to organise suitable surveillance by Party organisations over the behaviour of those expelled; it is necessary to keep them in mind, to know where they are working, in order to make it possible to spy on them.

* Oblast (Region) Communist Party

Quoted in Merle Fainsod, *Smolensk Under Soviet Rule*, Macmillan, 1959.

---

1 Judging by source D, what problems was a person likely to face as a result of being purged from the Party?
2 What do you think the writer meant by 'socially dangerous elements'? Which of the people listed in source B do you think risked being classified as 'socially dangerous elements'?
3 Bearing in mind that sources B, C and D are secret Party documents, and are available to historians only because they were captured during the Second World War, how reliable do you consider them as historical evidence? Explain your answer.

Being purged from the Party did not automatically lead to arrest by the NKVD, and many of the people arrested during the Great Purge of 1935–38 had never been Party members. People were arrested for an extraordinary variety of reasons: engineers, doctors and technicians for 'wrecking' activities; works managers for allowing the production of defective goods; peasants suspected of being kulaks (rich peasants); members of national minorities suspected of wanting independence from the Soviet Union; Trotskyites; friends and relations of Trotskyites. . . . The list was endless. Some of the fantastic crimes of which people were accused were described in 1935 by Andrei Vyshinski, the Prosecutor-General:

E How are people convicted? What are people convicted for? Here are a few examples. A woman cook failed to salt the dinner. She was prosecuted under Paragraph 111 (Par. 111 deals with 'failure to perform official duties' and with exceeding one's authority.) A kolkhoz* worker took a horse and went about his business; the horse was stolen; the kolkhoz worker was arrested under par. 111, although it would have been much fairer and simpler to have him make up for the value of the horse. A one-eyed foal was born in a kolkhoz; it was killed and eaten. The chairman of the kolkhoz was prosecuted for 'failure to protect' the young horse. A kolkhoz worker was prosecuted for reducing the sowing norm, even though the harvest turned out to be good; he was tried and convicted. The manager of a farm had pity on two calves and brought them indoors out of the frost. The calves' ears froze up, and the man was tried and convicted under par. 111. In January 1935 the Peoples' Court sentenced a certain Pankratov under pars. 109 and 111 of the Criminal Code for inflicting damages totalling 69 roubles on his kolkhoz. The accused had been sent into town to sell rye; instead of selling it at 26 or 27 roubles he sold it at 23 roubles. He was arrested and convicted for poor salesmanship.

* *a collective farm*

Quoted in David J. Dallin and Boris I. Nicolaevsky, *Forced Labour in Soviet Russia*, Hollis and Carter, 1948.

---

1 What can you learn from source E about peasant attitudes to the kolkhozy?
2 How does Vyshinski suggest that the law was applied with unnecessary harshness in some cases?

Some of the reasons why people were arrested during the Great Purge were bizarre. The great Soviet composer Dimitri Shostakovich described one such case in his memoirs, published in 1979:

F I'm not a historian. I could tell many tragic tales and cite many examples, but I won't do that. I will tell you about one incident, only one. It's a horrible story and every time I think about it, I grow frightened, and I don't want to remember it. Since time immemorial folk singers have wandered along the roads of the Ukraine. They're called *lirniki* and *banduristy* there. They were almost always blind men – why that is so, is another question that I won't go into, but briefly; it's traditional. The point is, they were always blind and defenceless people, but no one ever touched or hurt them. Hurting a blind man – what could be lower?

And then in the mid thirties the First All-Ukrainian Congress of *Lirniki* and *Banduristy* was announced, and all the folk singers had to gather and discuss what to do in the future. "Life is better, life is merrier" Stalin had said. The blind men believed it. They came to the Congress from all over the Ukraine, from tiny, forgotten villages. There were several hundred of them at the Congress, they say. It was a living museum, the country's living history; all its songs, all its music and poetry. And they were almost all shot, almost all those pathetic men killed.

Why was it done? Why the sadism – killing the blind? Just like that, so that they wouldn't get underfoot. Mighty deeds were being done there, complete collectivisation was under way, they had destroyed the kulaks as a class, and here were these blind men, walking around singing songs of dubious content. The songs weren't passed by the censors. And what kind of censorship can you have with blind men? You can't hand a blind man a corrected and approved text and you can't write him an order either. You have to tell everything to a blind man. That takes too long. And you can't file away a piece of paper, and there's no time anyway. Collectivisation. Mechanisation. It was easier to shoot them. And so they did.

From Solomon Volkov (ed.), *Testimony: The Memoirs of Dimitri Shostakovich* (translated by Antonina W. Bouis), Hamish Hamilton, 1979.

---

1 Why, according to Shostakovich, were the folk singers shot?
2 Shostakovich begins by stating 'I'm not a historian'. Why do you think he said this, and does it affect the value of his story as historical evidence?

We have found out a number of reasons why the Great Purge of 1935–38 was carried out, but none of them explain why so many people were arrested and killed. Nadezhda Mandelstam, wife of the poet Osip Mandelstam who died in a labour camp in 1938, offered an explanation in her memoirs, *Hope Against Hope*, published in 1975:

G They [the secret police] were not the least bit interested in real facts – all they wanted were lists of people to arrest, and these they got from their network of informers and the volunteers who brought them denunciations. To meet their quotas, all they needed were the names of people, not details about their comings and goings. During interrogations they always, as a matter of routine, collected 'evidence' against people whom they had no intention of arresting – just in case it was ever needed.

In the torture chambers of the Lubianka they were constantly adding to the dossiers of Ehrenburg, Sholokhov, Alexei Tolstoi* and others whom they had no intention of touching. . . . Wild inventions and monstrous accusations had become an end in themselves, and officials of the secret police applied all their ingenuity to them, as though revelling in the total arbitrariness of their power. . . .

* *Soviet writers who managed to stay in favour*

The principles and aims of mass terror have nothing in common with ordinary police work or with security. The only purpose of terror is intimidation. To plunge the whole country into a state of chronic fear the number of victims must be raised to astronomic levels, and on every floor of every building there must always be several apartments from which the tenants have suddenly been taken away. The remaining inhabitants will be model citizens for the rest of their lives. . . .

From Nadezhda Mandelstam, *Hope Against Hope: A Memoir* (translated by Max Hayward), Penguin Books, 1975.

---

1 Why, according to Nadezdha Mandelstam in source G, were so many people arrested during the Great Purge?
2 What, according to Nadezhda Mandelstam, was the purpose of the Great Purge?
3 Do any of the other sources in this chapter support her point of view?
4 Bearing in mind that her husband was arrested during the Great Purge, and died in a labour camp, is Nadezhda Mandelstam a biased witness of the Great Purge? If so, does this affect the value of source G as historical evidence? Explain your answer.

Despite the mass terror of the 1930s, at least some Soviet people were able to keep a black sense of humour. Source H is a joke that went the rounds in the mid-1930s:

H Polish rabbit: Why have you fled to Poland?
Russian rabbit: Because Stalin is preparing a bear hunt.
Polish rabbit: But you're not a bear.
Russian rabbit: No, but I can't prove it.

Quoted in J. N. Westwood, *Endurance and Endeavour: Russian History, 1812–1980*, Oxford University Press, 1981.

And source I is a cartoon drawn by a Soviet exile and published in Paris in 1938:

I

1 What point was the cartoonist in source I trying to make?
2 Does the fact that some Soviet citizens could joke about the Purge suggest that they weren't too worried by it? Explain your answer.

While Stalin was alive, most Soviet people did not dare to speak or write freely about the Great Purge; and many of those who acquired first-hand evidence of it died in the labour camps of the NKVD. Reliable evidence concerning the Great Purge is therefore not always easy to find, and anyone using the evidence that is available should start by questioning its reliability.

1 Do you have any reason to doubt the reliability or usefulness of any of the sources in this chapter? If so, why?
2 Bearing in mind the answer you have given to the last question, use the sources in this chapter as evidence to explain why so many Soviet people were expelled from the Communist Party and arrested by the secret police during the mid-1930s.

9 Down the road to war: international relations, 1931–39

During the late 1920s many people grew to believe that the world was entering a long period of peace. The international conflicts of the early 1920s had mostly been settled; the League of Nations had become an established feature of the world scene; all the major powers had renounced war by signing the Kellogg Pact in 1928; and a disarmament conference involving sixty nations was due to start in Geneva in 1932. Viscount Cecil, chief of the British delegation to the League of Nations Assembly, was one of those who foresaw a peaceful future for the world. In a speech to the Assembly on 10 September 1931, he said:

A I do not think that there is the slightest prospect of any war. I know – and history tells us – how rash it is to prophesy as to the future of international affairs; but, nevertheless, I do not believe there is anyone in this room who will contradict me when I say that there has scarcely ever been a period in the world's history when war seemed less likely than it does at present.

From The League of Nations, *Official Journal*, Special Supplement 93, 1931.

Regrettably, it took only a week for Viscount Cecil to be proved wrong. During the night of 18–19 September 1931, one member of the League of Nations, Japan, invaded the territory of a fellow member, China. It was the first of a series of acts of aggression during the 1930s that put the world on a road towards the Second World War of 1939–45. The documents in this chapter trace some of those steps on the road to war.

The Japanese invasion of Manchuria, in north-east China, in 1931 began with a shooting incident. To establish who was to blame for the incident, the League of Nations sent a Commission of Enquiry led by Lord Lytton to investigate. The Lytton Report, published in 1932, pieced together two different versions of how shooting began in the city of Mukden in Manchuria.

B According to the Japanese versions, Lieutenant Kawamoto, with six men under his command, was on patrol duty on the night of September 18th, practising defence exercises along the track of the South Manchuria Railway to the north of Mukden. They were proceeding southwards in the direction of Mukden. The night was dark but clear and the field of vision was not wide. When they reached a point at which a small road crosses the line, they heard the noise of a loud explosion a little way behind them. They turned and ran back, and after going about 200 yards they discovered that a portion of one of the rails on the down track had been blown out. . . . On arrival at the site of the explosion, the patrol was fired upon from the fields on the east side of the line. Lieutenant Kawamoto immediately ordered his men to . . . return the fire. The attacking body, estimated at five or six, then stopped firing and retreated northwards. The Japanese patrol at once started in pursuit and, having gone about 200 yards, they were again fired upon by a larger body, estimated at between three and four hundred. Finding himself in danger of being surrounded by this large force, Lieutenant Kawamoto then ordered one of his men ... to telephone (by means of a box telephone near the spot) to Battalion Headquarters at Mukden for reinforcements.

Lieutenant Kawamoto's patrol, [now] reinforced by Captain Kawashima's Company, was still sustaining the fire of the Chinese troops concealed in the tall Kaoliang grass, when the two Companies [of reinforcements] arrived from Mukden. Although his force was then only 500, and he believed the Chinese army in the North Barracks numbered 10,000, Lt. Col. Shinamoto at once ordered an attack on the Barracks. ... The attack was vigorously contested by the Chinese troops within, and there was fierce fighting for some hours. ... By 6 o'clock a.m. the entire barracks was captured at the cost of two Japanese privates killed and twenty-two wounded.

According to the Chinese version, the Japanese attack on the barracks was entirely unprovoked and came as a complete surprise. On the night of September 18th, all the soldiers of the 7th Brigade, numbering about 10,000, were in the North Barracks. As instructions had been received from Marshal Chang Hsueh-liang* on September 6th that special care was to be taken to avoid any clash with Japanese troops in the tense state of feeling at the time, the sentries at the walls of the Barracks were armed only with dummy rifles. ... The Japanese had been carrying out night manoeuvres around the barracks on the nights of September 14, 15, 16, 17. ... At 10 p.m. (of the 18th) the sound of a loud explosion was heard, immediately followed by rifle fire. This was reported over the telephone by the Chief of Staff to the Commanding Officer. ... While the Chief of Staff was still at the telephone, news was brought to him that the Japanese were attacking the barracks.

military governor and 'warlord' of Manchuria

Quoted in Sara R. Smith, *The Manchurian Crisis, 1931–32: A Tragedy in International Relations*, Columbia University Press, 1948.

---

1 On what points do the Japanese and Chinese versions of events agree? How do they differ?

2 Why do you think the Japanese force of 500 men was able to capture the Chinese barracks defended by 10,000 men, and yet sustain only 24 casualties?

3 How can you tell from source B that relations between Japan and China were already tense before this incident happened?

The Mukden Incident of 1931 was quickly followed by a full-scale invasion of the whole of Manchuria. By 1932 Japanese troops were in full control of the province, and poised to invade other, neighbouring provinces of China. The next blow to world peace was not struck in China, however, but in the African state of Ethiopia, which Italian forces invaded on 2 October 1935. Benito Mussolini, Fascist dictator of Italy, explained why he had ordered the invasion of Ethiopia in a remarkable radio broadcast to the Italian people. On the day of the invasion, wailing sirens and clanging church bells summoned more than twenty million Italians to town and village squares all over Italy, where huge loudspeakers relayed Mussolini's voice to them:

C Blackshirts of the revolution, men and women of all Italy, Italians scattered throughout the world, across the mountains and across the oceans, listen.

A solemn hour is about to strike in the history of the Fatherland. Twenty million Italians are at this moment gathered in squares throughout the whole of Italy. It is the most gigantic demonstration which the history of mankind records. Twenty millions, a single heart, a single will, a single decision. . . .

Not only is an army marching towards its objectives, but forty million Italians are marching in unison with this army, all united because there is an attempt to commit against them the blackest of all injustices, to rob them of a place in the sun. When in 1915 Italy united its lot with those of the Allies, how many shouts of admiration and how many promises! But after the common victory, to which Italy had brought the supreme contribution of 670,000 dead, 400,000 disabled, 1,000,000 wounded, when it came to sitting around the table of the mean peace, to us were left only the crumbs from the sumptuous colonial booty of others. . . .

At the League of Nations, instead of recognising the just rights of Italy, they dared to speak of sanctions*. Now, until there is proof to the contrary, I refuse to believe that the true people of France can associate themselves with sanctions against Italy. . . . Until there is proof to the contrary, I refuse to believe that the true people of Great Britain want to spill blood and push Europe on the road to catastrophe in order to defend an African country universally stamped as a barbarous country. . . .

* an economic boycott of a country.

At the same time, we must not pretend to know the eventualities of tomorrow. To sanctions of an economic character we will reply with our discipline, with our sobriety and with our spirit of sacrifice. To sanctions of a military character we will reply with orders of a military character. To acts of war we will reply with acts of war.

From The Royal Institute of International Affairs, *Documents on International Affairs*, 1935.

---

1 How does Mussolini justify the invasion of Ethiopia in this speech?
2 What do you think were his aims in making this radio speech?
3 Why did Mussolini refuse to believe that members of the League of Nations would take sanctions against Italy?
4 What does this speech tell you about the nature of Mussolini's Fascist government?

While the League of Nations argued about how to halt the Italian army in Ethiopia, Adolf Hitler, the dictator of Germany, struck another blow to peace by sending German troops into the Rhineland, the demilitarised zone of western Germany from which troops were banned by the Treaty of Versailles. William Shirer, an American journalist living in Berlin, listened to the speech which Hitler made to the German Reichstag, informing the deputies that the German army had entered the Rhineland. Shirer recorded what he saw and heard in his diary, which was published in 1941:

D Hitler began with a long harangue which he has often given before, but never tires of repeating, about the injustices of the Versailles Treaty and the peacefulness of Germans. Then his voice, which had been low and hoarse at the beginning, rose to a shrill, hysterical scream as he raged against Bolshevism.

'I will not have the gruesome Communist international dictatorship descend upon the German people!. . . I tremble for Europe at the thought of what would happen. . .' (Wild Applause).

Then, in a more reasoned voice, his argument that France's pact with Russia had invalidated the Locarno Treaty*. A slight pause and:

agreement made in 1925 between Germany, France and Belgium to respect each others' frontiers

'Germany no longer feels bound by the Locarno Treaty. In the interest of the primitive rights of its people to the security of their frontier and the safeguarding of their defence, the German government has re-established, as from today, the absolute and unrestricted sovereignty of the Reich in the demilitarised zone!'

Now the six hundred deputies, personal appointees all of Hitler, little men with big bodies and bulging necks and cropped hair and pouched bellies and brown uniforms and heavy boots, little men of clay in his fine hands, leap to their feet like automatons, their right arms upstretched in the Nazi salute, and scream 'Heil's', the first two or three wildly, the next twenty-five in unison, like a college yell. Hitler raises his hand for silence. It comes slowly. Slowly the automatons sit down. Hitler now has them in his claws. He appears to sense it. He says in a deep, resonant voice: 'Men of the German Reichstag!' The silence is utter. 'In this historic hour, when in the Reich's western provinces German troops are at this minute marching into their future peace-time garrisons. . . .'

He can go no further. It is news to this hysterical 'parliamentary' mob that German soldiers are already on their way into the Rhineland. All the militarism in their German blood surges to their heads. They spring, yelling and crying, to their feet. . . . Their hands are raised in slavish salute, their faces now contorted with hysteria, their mouths wide open, shouting, shouting, their eyes, burning with fanaticism, glued on the new god, the Messiah. . . .

From William Shirer, Berlin Diary: The Journal of a Foreign Correspondent, 1934–1941, Alfred A. Knopf, 1941.

1 What justifications does Hitler give for sending German troops into the demilitarised Rhineland?

2 What impression does Shirer create of (a) Hitler, and (b) the deputies of the Reichstag?

3 Bearing in mind (a) the style in which Shirer wrote this account, and (b) the year in which he published it, why might a historian suspect Shirer of biased reporting?

4 Does the bias in Shirer's reporting affect its value as historical evidence? Explain your answer.

5 Compare sources C and D. What similarities are there between (a) the content, (b) the style, and (c) the purposes of Hitler's and Mussolini's speeches?

The aggression of Japan, Italy and Germany between 1931 and 1936 led many people, particularly young people with left-wing political views, to believe that they should make a stand against these countries, which they called Fascist. When a civil war began in Spain in 1936 between pro-Fascist Nationalists and left-wing Republicans, more than 40,000 young people made their way to Spain to join volunteer International Brigades, fighting on the Republican side. One of them, a 26-year-old British sculptor named Jason Gurney, later described why he went to fight in Spain:

E The Spanish Civil War seemed to provide the chance for a single individual to take a positive and effective stand on an issue which seemed to be absolutely clear. Either you were opposed to the growth of Fascism and went out to fight against it, or you acquiesced in its crimes and were guilty of permitting its growth. There were many people who claimed it was a foreign quarrel and that nobody other than Spaniards should involve themselves in it, but for myself and many others like me it was a war of principle, and principles do not have national boundaries. By fighting against Fascism in Spain we would be fighting against it in our own countries, and every other. We felt that the victory of Fascism was inevitable. Mussolini had triumphed overnight, Hitler appeared to be irresistible, and there were similar leaders throughout the world.

In December 1936 I therefore decided I had a positive duty to go to Spain and join the International Brigades. . . .

From Jason Gurney, *Crusade in Spain*, Faber and Faber, 1974.

---

1 Judging by what you have read in sources C and D, suggest why Jason Gurney thought that 'the victory of Fascism was inevitable'.
2 In your own words, explain why Jason Gurney went to fight in Spain.

More than a third of the 40,000 young people who fought against Fascism in the Spanish Civil War were killed in action, but their sacrifice did not halt the aggression of the Fascist dictators. Between 1936 and 1939 Japan, Italy and Germany pursued their aims with increasing aggression, drawing together in a tripartite Axis Pact for mutual support in 1937.

The leaders of the countries most threatened by Axis. Pact aggression disagreed about how they should face up to the threat. Neville Chamberlain, Prime Minister of Britain from 1937 to 1940, followed a policy that his critics were soon calling 'appeasement'. Appeasement meant agreeing to whichever of Hitler's and Mussolini's demands seemed reasonable in order to prevent them taking what they wanted by force. Although appeasement meant strengthening the Axis powers, Chamberlain regarded this as a lesser threat to Britain and her Empire than going to war against the Axis.

Chamberlain's policy of appeasement was severely tested in the summer of 1938 when a major European crisis seemed certain to end in war. The crisis concerned the Sudetenland region of Czechoslovakia, shown here in source F.

F

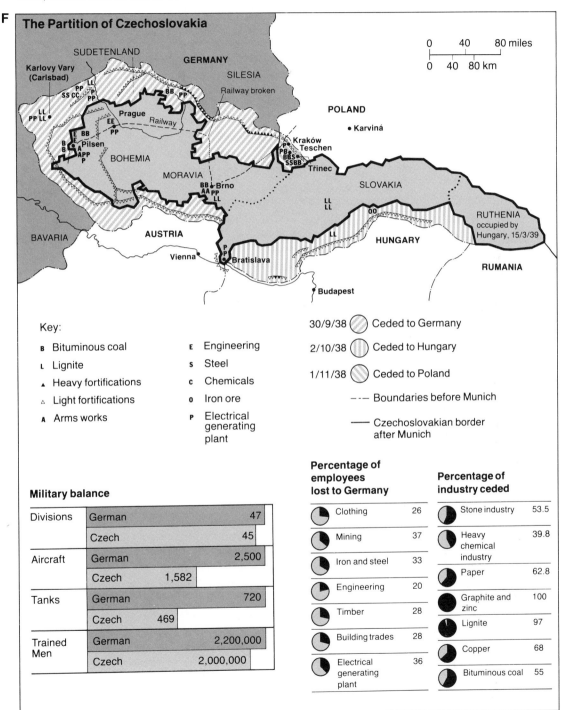

The Partition of Czechoslovakia

Key:

B Bituminous coal
L Lignite
▲ Heavy fortifications
△ Light fortifications
A Arms works

E Engineering
S Steel
C Chemicals
O Iron ore
P Electrical generating plant

30/9/38 Ceded to Germany
2/10/38 Ceded to Hungary
1/11/38 Ceded to Poland

--- Boundaries before Munich
—— Czechoslovakian border after Munich

Military balance

Divisions	German	47
	Czech	45
Aircraft	German	2,500
	Czech	1,582
Tanks	German	720
	Czech	469
Trained Men	German	2,200,000
	Czech	2,000,000

Percentage of employees lost to Germany

Clothing	26
Mining	37
Iron and steel	33
Engineering	20
Timber	28
Building trades	28
Electrical generating plant	36

Percentage of industry ceded

Stone industry	53.5
Heavy chemical industry	39.8
Paper	62.8
Graphite and zinc	100
Lignite	97
Copper	68
Bituminous coal	55

Based on *Purnell's History of the Twentieth Century*, BPC Publishing, 1968.

Around three million people living in the Sudetenland were German speaking. For some years a pro-Nazi Sudeten German Party had been carrying out a campaign of violence against the Czech government, demanding the separation of the Sudetenland from Czechoslovakia and its union with Germany. The Sudeten German campaign gave Hitler an excuse to prepare a military invasion of Czechoslovakia. Claiming that the Czech government was mistreating the Sudeten Germans, Hitler announced that the German army would enter the Sudetenland in order to restore order and to protect the rights of the Sudeten Germans.

Chamberlain attempted to halt the German invasion of the Sudetenland by appeasing Hitler, flying three times to Germany for private talks with him. The outcome of those talks was the Munich Agreement of 1938, transferring the Sudetenland to Germany. The reaction of the Czech government to the Munich Agreement can be seen in source G, a note from the Czech Foreign Minister, Jan Masaryk, to the British Government on 25 September 1938. The note should be studied in conjunction with the map (source F), which illustrates the terms of the Munich Agreement.

G My Government has now studied the document and the map. It is a *de facto* ultimatum of the sort usually presented to a vanquished nation and not a proposition to a sovereign state which has shown the greatest possible readiness to make sacrifices for the appeasement of Europe. . . . My Government is amazed at the contents of the memorandum. The proposals . . . deprive us of every safeguard for our national existence. We are to yield up large proportions of our carefully prepared defences and admit the German armies deep into our country before we have been able to organise it on the new basis or make any preparations for its defence. Our national and economic independence would automatically disappear. . . . My Government wishes me to declare in all solemnity that Herr Hitler's demands in their present form are absolutely and unconditionally unacceptable. . . .

Documents on British Foreign Policy 1919–1939, Third Series, vol. 2, HMSO, 1949.

---

1 What provides a country with (a) national independence, and (b) economic independence?
2 Using the information in source F, explain what Masaryk meant by saying that Czechoslovakia's 'national and economic independence would automatically disappear'.
3 According to source F, how did the Munich Agreement deprive Czechoslovakia of 'every safeguard of our national existence'?
4 Judging by source F, suggest other reasons why the Czech government thought the Munich Agreement was 'absolutely and unconditionally unacceptable'.

Critics of the policy of appeasement seemed to have been proved right in March 1939. Having gained control of the Sudetenland, the German army went on to invade the Czech provinces of Bohemia and Moravia. Czechoslovakia thus ceased to exist as an independent nation. In a speech in March 1939, Neville Chamberlain had this to say about it:

H It has been suggested that this occupation of Czecho-Slovakia was the direct consequence of the visit which I paid to Germany last autumn, and that since the result of these events has been to tear up the settlement that was arrived at at Munich, that proves that the whole circumstances of those visits were wrong. It is said that, as this was the personal policy of the Prime Minister, the blame for the fate of Czecho-Slovakia must rest on his shoulders. . . .

Well, I have never denied that the terms which I was able to secure at Munich were not those that I myself would have desired. But, as I explained then, I had to deal with no new problem. This was something that had existed ever since the Treaty of Versailles – a problem that ought to have been solved long ago if only the statesmen of the last twenty years had taken broader and more enlightened views of their duty. It had become like a disease which had been long neglected, and a surgical operation was necessary to save the life of the patient.

After all, the first and the most immediate object of my visit was achieved. The peace of Europe was saved; and, if it had not been for those visits, hundreds of thousands of families would today have been in mourning for the flower of Europe's best manhood. . . .

Really I have no need to defend my visits to Germany last autumn, for what was the alternative? Nothing that we could have done, nothing that France could have done, or Russia could have done could possibly have saved Czecho-Slovakia from invasion and destruction.

From *Documents Concerning German-Polish Relations and the Outbreak of Hostilities between Great Britain and Germany on September 3, 1939*, HMSO, 1939.

---

1 Why do you think Chamberlain's critics suggested that the German occupation of Czechoslovakia in March 1939 was the direct result of his policy of appeasement?
2 How does Chamberlain defend the policy of appeasement in this speech?
3 How convincing do you find Chamberlain's defence? Explain your answer.

The German occupation of Czechoslovakia convinced even the supporters of appeasement that stronger action would be needed to stop Hitler from striking again. And as it seemed that Poland was likely to be his next victim, the British and French governments agreed on 31 March 1939 to come to Poland's aid if she was attacked. Accordingly, when the German army invaded Poland five months later, on 1 September 1939, the British and French governments declared war on Germany.

Read source A and the introduction to this chapter again:
1 Why in 1931 did Viscount Cecil think 'there is not the slightest prospect of any war'?
2 Given that he thought it 'rash' to prophesy the future of international affairs, suggest why Viscount Cecil made this prophecy.
3 Using sources B to H make a list of reasons why the 1930s became a time of aggression in world affairs.

10 People at war: civilians in the Second World War, 1939–45

The World War of 1939–45 was a total war. This means that it involved not only the armed forces of the combatant countries, but also their civilian populations. In Britain and Germany and in China and Japan, for example, literally millions of townspeople spent the war years in fear of bombing from the air as enemy aircraft tried to wipe out their homes, their places of work and their means of transport. In countries under enemy occupation, millions of people were taken from their homes and forced into slave labour in distant lands. Millions more who resisted enemy occupation were executed by the occupiers as resistance fighters. And around six million Jewish civilians in countries occupied by Nazi Germany were murdered in an attempt to wipe out every Jew in Europe.

Of the fifty million people killed in the Second World War, over half were civilians. The names of the places where they suffered are today the symbols of total war; the bombed cities of Hiroshima, Dresden, Coventry; the extermination camps at Auschwitz, Belsen, Treblinka; besieged Leningrad, Warsaw, Chungking; the villages of Lidice and Oradour.

The sources in this chapter illustrate some of the ways in which civilians on both sides of the global conflict experienced total war. Inevitably, some of those experiences make disturbing reading.

The method of warfare which affected the greatest number of civilians was bombing from the air. Source A is a description of how people reacted to a bombing raid on London during the 'Blitz' of 1940. It was written by a member of Mass Observation, a social research organisation set up in 1937 to record accurate observations of everyday life in Britain:

A This record begins at 8.15 p.m., 7 September – inside a street shelter at Smithy Street, Stepney, East London again. Already about 35 people have crowded in. Some are sitting on stools or deckchairs, some standing.

At 8.15 p.m. a colossal crash, as if the whole street was collapsing; the shelter itself shaking. Immediately an ARP* helper, a nurse, begins singing lustily, in an attempt to drown out the noise – 'Roll out the barrel. . .!' while Mrs S, wife of a dyer and cleaner, screams:

'My house! It come on my house! My house is blown to bits!'

Her daughter, 25, begins to cry: 'Oh, is it true? Is our house really down?'

There are three more tremendous crashes. Women scream and there is a drawing together physically. Two sisters clasp one another; women huddle together. There is a feeling of breath being held; everyone waiting for more. No more. People stir, shift their positions, make themselves more comfortable.

Then, suddenly, a woman of 25 shouts at a younger girl:

'Stop leaning against that wall, you bloody fool! Like a bleeding lot of children! Get off it, you bastard . . . do you hear? Come off it . . . my God, we're going mad.'

* Air Raid Precautions, an organisation which enforced blackout regulations, gave air-raid warnings, etc.

People begin shouting at one another. Sophie, 30, screams at her mother: 'Oh, you get on my nerves, you do! You get on my nerves! Oh, shut up, you get on my nerves!'

Here the ARP helper tries once again to start some singing.

'Roll out the. . .' – she begins.

'Shut your bleedin' row!' shouts a man of 50. 'We got enough noise without you. . .' Outside the gunfire bursts forth again. It grows louder, and now the ARP girl begins walking up and down the shelter, singing and waggling her shoulders; a fine-looking girl, tall and handsome, with a lovely husky voice:

'There's a good time a'coming, though it's ever so far away. . . .'

Older woman (to young girl sitting beside her), 'Why don't *you* sing?'

'I can't! I don't want to! I can't!' cries the girl. 'I can't!. . . Oh, God. . .!'

The singer tries to get people to join in, but they won't. She gives up and sits down.

'My God,' says a young artisan, 'I want to laugh!'

Around midnight, a few people in the shelter are asleep but every time a bomb goes off, it wakes them. Several women are crying. At each explosion there is a burst of singing from the next shelter. Two men are arguing about the whereabouts of the last bomb.

Suddenly a girl cries out: 'I wish they'd bloody well stop talking and let me sleep! They talk such rot . . . such rot it is! That man, listen to him . . . he's got such a horrible voice! Tell him to stop. . . . Tell him I said he's to stop, he's got a horrible voice. . .!'

The girl's neighbour tries to calm her, urges her to try to sleep. No; she screams: 'It's no good! I'm ill! I think I'm going to die!'

By now the women with deck chairs are lying back in them wearily, rocking and groaning.

Woman of 60: 'If we ever live through this night, we have the good God above us to thank for it!'

Friend: 'I don't know if there is one, or he wouldn't let us suffer like this.'

From Tom Harrisson, *Living Through the Blitz*, Collins, 1976.

1　In general, what kinds of people were in the air-raid shelter?

2　Why do you think the ARP helper kept trying to start a sing-song, and why do you think most people refused to join in?

3　In general, how did people in the shelter react to the bombing?

4　The founder of Mass Observation (see source A) said that they should approach 'the study of Britons as if they were birds, emphasising seen behaviour or overheard conversation rather than interviews'. Bearing that comment in mind, consider the following questions:

(a)　Why do you think the observer in source A decided to make a record of this particular scene?

(b)　What does source A reveal about people's reactions to a bombing raid that could not be revealed by interviews?

(c)　How useful do you consider source A as evidence of how people reacted to bombing raids?

As the war went on, each side's bombing raids became more and more deadly. From 1942 to the end of the war, the Royal Air Force's Bomber Command carried out the 'area bombing' of population centres in Germany rather than of industrial and military targets. Area bombing was carried out by huge numbers of aircraft. Flying in formations of up to a thousand at a time, the bombers dropped a total of 482,437 tonnes of explosives on German towns and cities between January 1942 and the end of the war in May 1945. Sources B and C show some of the effects of an area bombing raid on Darmstadt by 218 Lancaster bombers on the night of 11 November 1944. They are taken from a series of interviews recorded by Darmstadt citizens twenty years after the raid, and published in a book of survivors' accounts. The first is from Martha Gros who remembered that:

B There was a dreadful crash, the walls shook, we heard masonry cracking and collapsing, and the crackle of flames. . . . About thirty seconds later there was a second terrible explosion, the cellar door flew open, and I saw, bathed in a brilliant light, the staircase to the cellar collapsing and a river of fire pouring down. I shouted 'Let's get out!'. . . . I dropped my cashbox and pulled the others with me. We climbed through the hole leading to the back. . . . More bombs were already falling into the garden. We crouched low, each of us beating out the small flames flickering on the clothes of the one in front. Phosphorus clung to the trees and dripped down on us. . . . The heat was terrible. Burning people raced past like live torches, and I listened to their unforgettable final screams. . . .

(The next day) It was even more unreal than the previous night. Not a bird, not a green tree, no people, nothing but corpses. . . . We climbed over the wreckage into the garden and proceeded to the burnt-out cellar. The ashes were almost two feet deep. I found the place where I had dropped the cash box, picked it up and opened it. The 1,000 Reichsmark note which I had saved for emergencies was a heap of ashes. The little boxes of jewellery had been burned. The best piece, a large emerald, had cracked. Around our safe lay large lumps of melted silver, and in the wine racks, there were melted bottles hanging in bizarre long ribbons. For this to have happened the temperature must have been something like 1,700 degrees.

From Klaus Schmidt, *Die Brandnacht*, Darmstadt, 1965.

Source C is from another citizen of Darmstadt, Jacob Schultz, who remembered that:

C One was afraid of losing one's reason. People from the rescue service were collapsing into nervous hysteria. It was a privilege to have a coffin, or the means to make one oneself. Most of the bodies were put on a lorry or wheeled in little handcarts to the mass graves in the cemetery.

The hospitals were crammed. All preparations counted for nothing. You could travel without a ticket on the train, bicycle on the pavements. There were no windows in the trains, no schools, no doctors, no post, no telephone. One felt completely cut off from the world. To meet a friend who survived was a wonderful experience. There was no water, no light, no fire. A candle was of priceless value. Little children collected wood from the ruins for cooking. Every family dug its own latrine in the garden. There was no more absolute ownership of anything. Many people moaned about their losses, yet others seemed almost relieved by their freedom from possessions. This had suddenly become a city of proletarians. . . .

From Klaus Schmidt, *Die Brandnacht*, Darmstadt, 1965.

---

1 Using sources B and C as evidence, describe in your own words the effects of 'area bombing' on the city of Darmstadt.
2 Judging by source B, to which social class did Martha Gros belong? Quote from the source to support your answer.
3 In source C, what does the term 'proletarian' mean? How does source B support the view in source C that Darmstadt 'had suddenly become a city of proletarians'?
4 Compare sources B and C, which were recorded in interviews twenty years after the event, with source A, which was recorded at the time it happened. Do you think sources B and C are any less useful as historical evidence because of this? Explain your answer.

In the air-raid described in sources B and C, 8,433 Darmstadt citizens were killed, 4,064 out of 8,401 houses were destroyed completely, and 70,000 people forced to leave their dwellings. 49,200 people fled from the city as refugees. The man who organised the raid, Air Chief Marshal Sir Arthur Harris, later wrote in his memoirs that:

D Bombing proved a comparatively humane method. For one thing, it saved the flower of the youth of this country and of our Allies from being mown down by the artillery in the field, as it was in Flanders in the war of 1914–1918.

Quoted in Max Hastings, *Bomber Command*, Dial Press/James Wade, 1979.

---

1 What arguments can you produce for and against this point of view?
2 Which argument do you find most convincing?

While townspeople in Britain and Germany cowered in air-raid shelters and cellars during the war, country people in the lands occupied by Nazi Germany experienced a different and even more upsetting disruption of their lives. One of the main aims of the Nazi conquest of Europe was to gain 'lebensraum', or 'living space', for Germany. In the most fertile areas, or in strategically important regions, this involved the mass expulsion of non-German people and their replacement with German or pro-German settlers. Source E is a description of a mass expulsion which took place in 1943 in the village of Tarnogrod in south-east Poland. The description was given by one of the villagers in evidence in 1946 to the Central Commission for the Investigation of German Crimes in Poland.

E On June 29, every one lost the last hope if he ever had any; the action was about to start. Cars packed with men arrived from neighbouring villages. . . . The posting of guards on roads, fields and in woods made escape impossible. Next day, on June 30, people awoke and peeped from their courtyards like hunted beasts. Farm work was not resumed for several days. . . .

About 6 o'clock a.m. inhabitants of the most distant streets were driven to the square. They were frightened and prepared for all eventuality. The crowd of victims increased on the market place. An SS-officer stood up in his car and said to the assembled:

'Poles! You will leave this area. You will be resettled in the territories inhabited by purely Polish population. Here the Ukrainians will be left in order to avoid the inconveniences of a mixed population. You have one hour to go home and pack your belongings. You are allowed to take 10 kg of luggage per person. In one hour everybody must be here again.'

The crowd dispersed and small groups of people hurried home to take some property.

One hour later all were again at the market place. Those who resisted were pushed by young SS-men. Some shots were heard. It rained and people were soaked. In spite of the summer weather they shivered. Women clasped in arms their frightened babies. . . .

At noon people began to be herded into lorries. Women and children were separated from their husbands, fathers and brothers. After the painful farewells the division of food was made and the women were brutally crammed into carts made to move faster by beating. . . . Before the start to an unknown destination they made the sign of the cross. The loading was not an easy thing to do since there were no men to help. A sick woman dropped an infant. After the women were loaded it was the turn of the men. Only those were left who could be of some use to the Germans and their allies, the Ukrainians. . . .

Later at night all quieted down. Only cattle mooed – they had not been watered this day – and the horses neighed. Sometimes the sound of axes and the breaking open of a door was heard, or a tumult made by robbers. It was the local Ukrainians who divided among themselves the spoil.

From The Central Committee for Investigation of German Crimes in Poland, *German Crimes in Poland*, vol. 2, Warsaw, 1947.

---

1 How much of their property were the villagers allowed to take with them? What do you think they were most likely to take with them, and what would most of them have to leave behind?

2 Why were the Ukrainians not expelled from the village?

3 In what ways was the experience of mass expulsion similar to the experience of townspeople in air-raids?

In every country occupied by the Germans during the Second World
War, groups of civilians joined together to resist them with every
means at their disposal. They carried out acts of sabotage, such as
blowing up railways and bridges, carried out assassinations, collected
information for the Allies, published anti-German propaganda, and
helped Allied airmen who had been shot down to get back home.
Partisans took tremendous risks in their resistance work and many
were captured. Those who were captured were usually executed, often
after being tortured to extract information about their fellow partisans.
Source F is a painting titled 'The Partisan's Mother' by the Soviet artist
Gerassimov. It was painted in 1942 when much of the western USSR
was occupied by the Germans.

F

1 Describe the situation portrayed in the painting.
2 What impression does the painter create of (a) the German, (b) the captured partisan, and (c) the
partisan's mother?
3 What message do you think the painter was trying to convey?

In Leningrad, the USSR's second city, civilians were subjected to a prolonged form of suffering – the siege of their city for nearly 900 days, from September 1941 to January 1944. Some of the effects of the siege were described by Captain Vishnevsky, a Soviet naval officer, in conversation with a journalist, Alexander Werth, in September 1943:

G At that time (winter 1941–42) . . . we were all very hungry. To walk up to the third floor was agony. You'd stop a dozen times before getting there. But people didn't complain. They never looted bakeries. Many thousands died quietly every week. The Komsomol* did all it could to keep people's morale up. They would drop in on people who were obviously going to pieces and say, 'Look here, old man, it wouldn't be a bad thing if you had a wash and a shave'. . . .

* Communist Youth League

There was a terrible fuel shortage, of course. One of the most extraordinary stunts of the blockade was this one. There is a place in the port of Leningrad where for half a century or more the coal ships from Cardiff used to be unloaded. As you know, when coal is unloaded there is always a certain amount of waste – the stuff drops into the water. Well, large holes were cut in the ice, and divers went down and worked for many days in the icy waters; and they brought to the surface 4,000 or 5,000 tons of coal! Those were the sorts of expedient to which we were reduced. . . .

Fearful things were happening all the time. There were dead bodies all over the place. Cats and dogs had disappeared completely. I knew an elderly artist who strangled his cat and ate it. Even last summer I remember taking some small children out into the country, and a little girl began to scream in terror: 'There's a German! There's a German!' What she saw was a pig. She had never seen a pig before, except on war posters. A lot of our children have never seen even a cat or a dog.

From Alexander Werth, *Leningrad*, Hamish Hamilton, 1944.

---

1 List the physical hardships suffered by the people of Leningrad during the siege of their city.

2 Judging by source G, how effective was the German siege? Explain your answer.

The hardships and horrors experienced by people at war from 1939 to 1945 came in an infinite variety of forms. In addition to the experiences described in this chapter, we must remember the appalling suffering of the Jewish people shown in chapter 7 (pages 46–54). In the light of so much suffering, it is perhaps not surprising that, when the war was over, the people who had suffered most wanted to take revenge on those who had caused the suffering. Source H, a photograph taken in France in 1945 by Robert Capa, reflects some of the hatred left at the end of the war. A young mother, accused of collaborating with the Germans who occupied France, has had her head forcibly shaved, and is being driven out of the town of Chartres.

H

1 Describe in as much detail as you can the situation depicted in the photograph.
2 What impression does the photographer create of (a) the young mother, and (b) the townspeople surrounding her?
3 Is it possible to tell from the photograph whether the photographer sympathised with the mother or with the crowd? Explain your answer.

1 Using sources A to G as evidence, explain why so many civilians died in the Second World War.
2 Historians have written of the extermination of the Jews during the War as 'the greatest single crime in history', as 'one of mankind's most extreme experiences of horror', and that 'there are few more ghastly pages in history', and so on. For what reasons, in your opinion, can the extermination of the Jews be considered a worse crime than the other horrors described in this chapter – area bombing, mass deportation, starvation, murder and torture?

11 Cold War, containment, confrontation: East–West relations after 1945

The USA, Britain and the USSR spent the last four years of the Second World War as partners in a 'Grand Alliance'; and at the war's end in 1945, all three shared in victory over Nazi Germany and Imperial Japan. Yet within the next two years, the war-time partners had split into two camps, each fearing and mistrusting the other. This state of mutual fear and mistrust, which the American financier Bernard Baruch named the Cold War, lasted for more than twenty years. On several occasions it threatened to develop into a new global war. Even after the fears and tensions of the Cold War eased in the late 1960s, relations between East and West remained uneasy. Some people today still believe that a major war between the two will eventually take place. What accounts for this extraordinary state of tension between the world's largest nations and their allies?

Back in 1848 Karl Marx and Friedrich Engels issued their Communist Manifesto, which began with the words 'A spectre is haunting Europe – the spectre of Communism'. Exactly a century later, United States President Truman and his advisers believed that Communism was not only haunting Europe, but had already possessed large parts of it. The map in source A shows some of the reasons why they thought so.

A

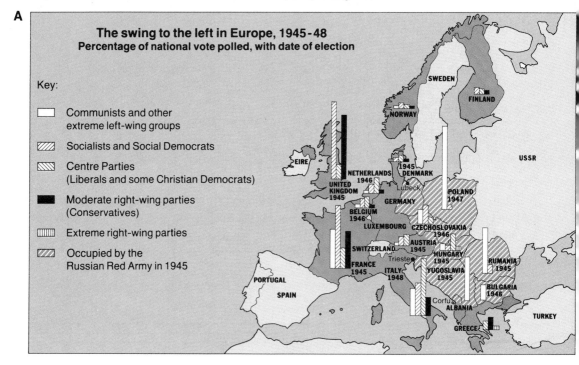

1 In which countries had Communists gained a majority in elections by 1948?
2 In which other countries were left-wing parties powerful by 1948?
3 In what other ways does the map suggest that 'the spectre of Communism' was haunting Europe in 1948?

In eight of the nations shown on the map, there was an extra factor which alarmed Truman and his advisers: the presence of the Soviet Red Army, which had occupied those countries after liberating them from Nazi rule. Winston Churchill, Prime Minister of Britain, explained why this worried him in a message to Truman on 12 May 1945 – less than a week after the defeat of Germany:

B . . . what is to happen about Russia? I have always worked for friendship with Russia, but like you, I feel deep anxiety because of . . . the combination of Russian power and the territories under their control or occupied, coupled with the Communist technique in so many other countries, and above all their power to maintain very large armies in the field for a long time. What will be the position in a year or two, when the British and American armies have melted . . . when we may have a handful of divisions . . . and when Russia may choose to keep two or three hundred on active service?

An iron curtain is drawn down upon their front. We do not know what is going on behind. There seems little doubt that the whole of the regions east of the line Lübeck-Trieste-Corfu will soon be completely in their hands.

From Barton J. Bernstein and Allen J. Matusow (eds.), *The Truman Administration: A Documentary History*, Harper and Row, 1966.

---

1 In your own words, explain Churchill's three reasons for feeling 'deep anxiety' about the future behaviour of the USSR.
2 How does source A support Churchill's view that all the land east of 'the line Lübeck-Trieste-Corfu' would soon be completely in Soviet hands?
3 Suggest what Churchill meant by 'an iron curtain is drawn down upon their front'.

One of the countries whose future worried Churchill was Greece, where a civil war between Communist and Royalist forces had begun in 1944. To prevent a Communist victory, the British government supplied the Royalists with troops, arms and money. At the same time it gave economic aid to neighbouring Turkey. In February 1947, however, the British government informed President Truman that it could no longer afford the cost of aid to Greece and Turkey. And without that aid, it was certain that the Communists would soon win the Greek civil war. Rather than allow that to happen, Truman asked the United States Congress to give $400 million in aid to the two nations in order to contain the spread of Communism. That policy of containing Communism soon became known as the Truman Doctrine:

C Mr President, Mr Speaker, Members of the Congress of the United States: . . .

The United States has received from the Greek Government an urgent appeal for financial and economic assistance. . . .

Greece is not a rich country. Lack of sufficient natural resources has always forced the Greek people to work hard to make both ends meet. Since 1940 this industrious and peace-loving country has suffered invasion, four years of cruel enemy occupation, and bitter internal strife.

When forces of liberation entered Greece they found that the retreating Germans had destroyed virtually all the railways, roads, port facilities, communications, and merchant marine. More than a thousand villages had been burnt. Eighty five per cent of the children were tubercular. Livestock, poultry and draft animals had almost disappeared. Inflation had wiped out practically all savings.

As a result of these tragic conditions, a militant minority, exploiting human want and misery, was able to create political chaos which, until now, has made economic recovery impossible. . . .

The very existence of the Greek state is today threatened by the terrorist activities of several thousand armed men, led by Communists, who defy the Government's authority. . . .

From The Royal Institute of International Affairs, *Documents on International Affairs 1947–48*, Oxford University Press, 1952.

---

1 How does Truman explain the spread of Communism in Greece?
2 What impression of the Greek Communists does Truman create?

Later in the same speech, Truman said:

D At the present moment in world history nearly every nation must choose between alternative ways of life. The choice is too often not a free one.

One way of life is based upon the will of the majority, and is distinguished by free institutions, representative government, free elections, guaranties of individual liberty, freedom of speech and religion, and freedom from political oppression.

The second way of life is based upon the will of a minority forcibly imposed upon the majority. It relies upon terror and oppression, a controlled press and radio, fixed elections, and the suppression of personal freedoms.

I believe that it must be the policy of the United States to support free peoples who are resisting attempted subjugation by armed minorities or by outside pressures.

I believe that we must help free peoples to work out their own destinies in their own way.

I believe that our help should be primarily through economic and financial aid which is essential to economic stability and orderly political processes. . . .

I therefore ask the Congress to provide authority for assistance to Greece and Turkey in the amount of $400,000,000 for the period ending June 30 1948. . . .

From The Royal Institute of International Affairs, *Documents on International Affairs, 1947–48*, Oxford University Press, 1952.

---

1 Which country or countries do you think Truman had in mind when he spoke of 'The second way of life . . . based upon the will of a minority'? Suggest why he did not name such countries.
2 How does Truman suggest that Greece was under threat from such countries?
3 Why did Truman think that economic and financial aid was likely to be effective?

The $400 million which Congress voted for Greece and Turkey was a drop in the ocean compared with what followed. Three months after Truman announced his 'Doctrine' to Congress, the US Secretary of State, General George C. Marshall, announced a much more ambitious plan of economic aid to the whole of Europe. In a speech at Harvard University on 5 June 1947, Marshall said:

E I need not tell you gentlemen that the world situation is very serious. . . .

The truth of the matter is that Europe's requirements for the next three or four years of foreign foods and other essential products – principally from America – are so much greater than her present ability to pay that she must have substantial economic help, or face economic, social and political deterioration of a very grave character. . . .

It is logical that the United States should do whatever it is able to do to assist in the return of normal economic health in the world, without which there can be no political stability and no assured peace. Our policy is directed not against any country or doctrine but against hunger, poverty, desperation and chaos. Its purpose should be the revival of a working economy in the world so as to permit the emergence of political and social conditions in which free institutions can exist.

From Barton J. Bernstein and Allen J. Matusow (eds.), *The Truman Administration: A Documentary History*, Harper and Row, 1966.

1 Why, according to Marshall, was Europe facing serious economic difficulties in 1947?
2 What do you think Marshall meant by saying that Europe faced 'economic, social and political deterioration of a very grave character' as a result of those difficulties?
3 Why did Marshall think that the United States should be involved in these European problems?
4 Why might it be suggested that Marshall's policy was directed against another country or doctrine, even though he denies this?

The Soviet government denounced both the Truman Doctrine and the Marshall Plan, and prevented the East European states under its control from accepting any of the $17,000 million which the United States gave to Europe over the next four years. In response to the Truman Doctrine, the Soviet newspaper *Izvestia* said:

F We are now witnessing a fresh intrusion of the USA into the affairs of other states. American claims to leadership in international affairs grow parallel with the growing appetite of the American quarters concerned. But the American leaders . . . fail to reckon with the fact that the old methods of the colonisers and diehard politicians have outlived their time and are doomed to failure. In this lies the chief weakness of Truman's message.

From The Royal Institute of International Affairs, *Documents on International Affairs, 1947–48*, Oxford University Press, 1952.

And in October 1947, the Manifesto of Cominform, the Communist Information Bureau that the USSR created that year to co-ordinate the activities of Communist parties in the Eastern European countries, stated that:

G The Truman-Marshall Plan is only a constituent part, the European, of the general plan of the world expansionist policy carried out by the United States in all parts of the world. The plan of economic and political enslavement of Europe by American imperialism is supplemented by plans for the economic and political enslavement of China, Indonesia and South America.

From The Royal Institute of International Affairs, *Documents on International Affairs, 1947–48*, Oxford University Press, 1952.

---

1 Why, according to sources F and G, did the Soviet government reject both the Truman Doctrine and the Marshall Plan?
2 What criticisms of the United States government's foreign policy are made in sources F and G?

In this growing atmosphere of mistrust between the USSR and the Western Allies, political leaders on both sides tended to interpret each other's decisions in the worst possible light. So when, in 1948, the Soviet army occupying Eastern Germany closed the roads, railways and waterways that linked West Berlin with the Western zones of Germany, the commander of the American forces in Germany said:

H We have lost Czechoslovakia. Norway is threatened. We retreat from Berlin. When Berlin falls, Western Germany will be next. . . . If we withdraw our position in Berlin, Europe is threatened. . . . Communism will run rampant.

From General L. Clay, *Decision in Germany*, Heinemann, 1950.

The Soviet blockade of Western Berlin lasted for eleven months. The Western Allies were able to break the blockade only by organising a massive daily airlift of supplies into the city. The whole experience forced the Western Allies to make a number of important decisions about their future relations with the USSR, and about how they should deal with such situations in the future. One decision which they made in the wake of the Berlin blockade was to form a new military defence structure. The North Atlantic Treaty, signed on 4 April 1949, stated that:

I The Parties to this Treaty (Belgium, Canada, Denmark, France, Iceland, Italy, Luxemburg, Netherlands, Norway, Portugal, United Kingdom and the United States) reaffirm their faith in the purposes and principles of the Charter of the United Nations and their desire to live in peace with all peoples and all governments.

They are determined to safeguard the freedom, common heritage and civilisation of their peoples, founded on the principles of democracy, individual liberty and the rule of law.

They seek to promote stability and well-being in the North Atlantic area. . . .

The Parties agree that an armed attack against one or more of them in Europe or North America shall be considered an attack against them all; and consequently they agree that, if such an armed attack occurs, each of them ... will assist the Party or Parties so attacked by taking forthwith, individually and in concert with the other Parties, such action as it deems necessary, including the use of armed force, to restore and maintain the security of the North Atlantic area. . . .

From *Keesings Contemporary Archives*, Longman, 1949.

1 The USSR described the North Atlantic Treaty Organisation as a 'weapon of an aggressive Anglo-American bloc in Europe ... aimed at the establishment of Anglo-American world domination'. Taking your information from source I,

  (a) shade in the member countries of NATO on a copy of the outline map below,

  (b) explain why you think the Soviet Union described NATO in this way, and

  (c) counter the Soviet view with an argument that might be put forward by a supporter of NATO.

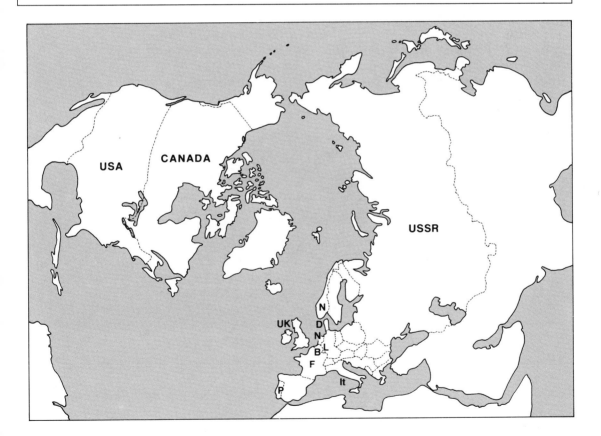

Soon after the North Atlantic Treaty was signed, the Berlin Blockade and the Greek Civil War both came to an end. The arena of the Cold War then shifted from Europe to the Far East when war broke out in Korea. It returned abruptly to Europe in 1961, and again the scene was Berlin.

Berlin, the capital of the Communist German Democratic Republic set up in 1949, was still a divided city. West Berlin was partly controlled by the British, French and Americans, whereas East Berlin was still a Soviet zone. By 1961, about a thousand East Germans were escaping each day into West Berlin and from there into West Germany. Many were skilled workers whom the Democratic Republic could not afford to lose. On the night of 12–13 August 1961, Soviet and East German 'shock workers' built a barrier between East and West Berlin to stop this exodus of refugees. Source J, a photograph taken in West Berlin in 1966, shows part of the barrier which they created. The propaganda poster behind the barbed wire says: 'Concentration camp builder Lubke (*President of West Germany*) how long are you going to go on telling lies?'

J

1 Study the photograph carefully, then describe exactly how the barrier between East and West Berlin was constructed.
2 The government of the German Democratic Republic (GDR) claimed that the purpose of the barrier was to stop Western spies and agents crossing into East Berlin and the GDR. How convincing do you find this explanation? Explain your answer.
3 How does everyday life appear to have been affected by the building of the Berlin Wall?
4 Why might East Berliners, such as the writer of the poster, have said that the Berlin Wall made West Berlin into a 'concentration camp'?
5 Suggest what the purpose of the poster was.

By far the most dangerous episode in the Cold War happened in Cuba in October 1962. Photographs taken by United States reconnaissance aircraft showed that rocket sites were being built on the island. The rockets were Soviet ones, and capable of striking at most major American cities. In a radio broadcast on 22 October, United States President Kennedy stated that:

K The purpose of these bases can be none other than to provide a nuclear strike capability against the Western Hemisphere. . . .

Acting, therefore, in the defence of our own security and that of the entire Western Hemisphere . . . I have directed that the following initial steps be taken immediately.

First: to halt this offensive build-up, a strict quarantine on all offensive military equipment under shipment to Cuba is being initiated. All ships of any kind bound for Cuba from whatever nation or port will, if found to contain cargoes of offensive weapons, be turned back. . . .

Second: I have directed the continued and close surveillance of Cuba and the military build-up. . . . Should these offensive military preparations continue, thus increasing the threat to the hemisphere, further action will be justified. I have directed the armed forces for any eventualities. . . .

Third: it shall be the policy of this nation to regard any nuclear missile launched from Cuba against any nation in the Western Hemisphere as an attack by the Soviet Union on the United States, requiring a full retaliatory response upon the Soviet Union. . . .

I call upon Chairman Khrushchev to halt and eliminate this clandestine, reckless and provocative threat to world peace and to stable relations between our two nations. . . .

From *Keesings Contemporary Archives, vol XIII*, Longman, 1962.

---

1 Explain what Kennedy meant by 'a strict quarantine on all offensive military equipment under shipment to Cuba'.
2 What risks do you think there were in imposing such a quarantine?
3 Many people following the news in 1962 feared that the Cuban Missile Crisis would develop into a full-scale nuclear war between the USA and USSR. Which parts of Kennedy's statement in source J do you think encouraged such fears?

In reply, Chairman Khrushchev of the USSR sent a long letter to Kennedy on 27 October 1962. A key passage in the letter read as follows:

L How are we, the Soviet Union, our Government, to assess . . . the fact that you have surrounded the Soviet Union with military bases; have disposed military bases literally around our country; have stationed your rocket armament there? This is no secret . . .

Your rockets are situated in Britain, situated in Italy, and are aimed against us. Your rockets are situated in Turkey. You are worried by Cuba. You say that it worries you because it is a distance of 90 miles by sea from the coast of America, but Turkey is next to us. Our sentries walk up and down and look at each other. . . .

I therefore make this proposal: we agree to remove from Cuba those means which you regard as offensive means; we agree to carry this out and make a pledge to the United Nations. Your representatives will make a declaration to the effect that the United States, considering the uneasiness and anxiety of the Soviet State, will remove its similar means from Turkey.

From *Keesings Contemporary Archives, vol XIII*, Longman, 1962.

President Kennedy rejected this remarkable offer, but continued to negotiate for a peaceful solution to the crisis. This came on 28 October when the USSR agreed to remove its missiles from the island and not to install any more. In return, Kennedy lifted the blockade of Cuba.

---

1 Do you think that Khrushchev's letter (source L) makes a fair point? Explain your answer.
2 Why do you think Kennedy refused to negotiate on Khrushchev's offer?

The Cuban Missile Crisis brought the world close to a third world war, and the fears that this aroused had a sobering effect on all the parties involved. Although the USA and the USSR continued to look at each other with the deepest suspicion, each took steps to ensure that such a confrontation could not happen so easily again. With the improvement of communications between Washington and Moscow, and with the signing of a treaty banning the testing of nuclear weapons in the atmosphere, the Cold War began slowly to unfreeze in the mid 1960s.

Using sources A to K in this chapter as evidence, explain what caused
1 the Americans and their allies to mistrust the USSR, and
2 the USSR and its allies to mistrust the USA.

12 The wind of change:
African independence movements after 1945

In October 1945 a group of young and little-known Africans calling themselves the Fifth Pan-African Congress met in the town hall of Chorlton-on-Medlock, a suburb of Manchester. Although these young men represented most of the territories of Africa, few newspapers reported the resolution which they passed:

A We are determined to be free. We want education. We want the right to earn a decent living, the right to express our thoughts and emotions, to adopt and create forms of beauty. We demand for Black Africa autonomy and independence. We will fight in every way we can for freedom, democracy and social betterment.

Quoted in Colin Legum, *Pan Africanism: a Short Political Guide*, Pall Mall Press, 1962.

The European empires which claimed to own the territories where these men lived were not prepared to agree to such demands. The policy of the British government, for example, was plainly stated in a White Paper in 1948:

B The central purpose of British colonial policy ... is to guide the colonial territories to responsible self-government within the Commonwealth in conditions that ensure to the people concerned both a fair standard of living and freedom from oppression in any quarter.

Quoted in Stewart Easton, *The Twilight of European Colonialism*, Methuen, 1961.

---

1 Which of the demands of the Pan-African Congress in source A could have been satisfied by the policy outlined in source B?
2 Which of the demands in source A could not have been satisfied by the policy outlined in source B? Explain both your answers.

Many Africans in Britain's colonial territories found that the pace at which Britain was guiding them to 'responsible self-government' was too slow, and gave their support to nationalist groups which were prepared to fight for independence. In Kenya, for example, one of the men who had attended the Pan-African Congress in 1945, Jomo Kenyatta, found an enthusiastic following among the Kikuyu people who had been expelled from their best land, the White Highlands, to make way for white British farmers. In source C, Karari Njama, a Kenyan schoolteacher, describes how he became involved in the struggle for his country's independence:

C It was 26 July 1952 and I sat in the Nyeri Showgrounds packed in with a crowd of over 30,000 people. The Kenya African Union was holding a rally and it was presided over by Jomo Kenyatta. He talked first of LAND. In the Kikuyu country, nearly half the people are landless and have an earnest desire to acquire land so that they can have something to live on. Kenyatta pointed out that there was a lot of land lying idly in the country and only the wild game enjoy that, while Africans are starving of hunger. . . .

The other point that Jomo Kenyatta stressed during the meeting was African FREEDOM. He raised the K.A.U. flag to symbolise African government. He said Kenya must be freed from colonial exploitation. Africans must be given freedom of speech, freedom of movement, freedom of worship and freedom of press. . . .

I was struck by its [the flag's] red colour in the middle of black and green. . . . When Kenyatta returned to the platform for the third time, after a few other speakers, he explained the flag. He said, 'Black is to show that this is for black people. Red is to show that the blood of an African is the same colour as the blood of a European, and green is to show that when we were given this country by God it was green, fertile and good, but now you see the green is below the red and suppressed.' (Tremendous applause.)

From Donald L. Barnett and Karari Njama, *Mau Mau From Within*, Macgibbon and Kee, 1966.

---

1 Judging by source C, what were the main complaints of the Kenya African Union about British colonial rule?
2 What further light is thrown on British colonial rule in Kenya by sources B and I in chapter 1 of this book (pages 1 and 5)?

In their struggle for freedom from British rule, many of the Kikuyu joined an underground organisation which the British derisively named Mau Mau, a Kikuyu word meaning 'greedy eating'. Between 1952 and 1959 Mau Mau used the ancient Kikuyu custom of oath-taking to build up a massive following. In source D, Karari Njami describes the oath he took when he joined Mau Mau in 1952:

D We were harassed to take out our coats, money, watches, shoes, and any other European metal we had in our possession. Then the oath administrator, Githinji Mwrari – who had painted his fat face with white chalk – put a band of raw goat's skin on the right hand wrist of each one of the seven persons who were to be initiated. We were then surrounded by goats' small intestines on our shoulders and feet. . . . Then Githinji pricked our right hand middle finger with a needle until it bled. . . . He then took a Kikuyu gourd containing blood and with it made a cross on our foreheads and on all important joints saying, 'May this blood mark the faithful and brave members of the Gikuyu and Mumbi Unity*; may this same blood warn you that if you betray our secrets or violate the oath, our members will come and cut you into pieces at the joints marked by this blood.'. . .

* the Kikuyu name for the Mau Mau organisation

We then swore: 'I (Karari Njama) swear before God and before all the people present here that. . .

1. I shall never reveal this secret of the K.C.A.* oath to . . . any person who is not a member of our society. If I ever reveal it may this oath kill me! (Repeated after each vow while biting the chest meat of a billy goat held together with the heart and lungs.)

2. I shall always help any member of our society who is in difficulty or need of help.

3. If I am ever called, during the day or night, to do any work for this society, I shall obey.

4. I shall on no account ever disobey the leaders of this society.

5. If I am ever given arms or ammunition to hide, I shall do so.

6. I shall always give money or goods to this society when called on to do so.

7. I shall never sell land to a European or an Asian.

8. I shall not permit intermarriage between Africans and the white community. . . .

13. I shall never drink European manufactured beer or [smoke] cigarettes.

14. I shall never spy on or otherwise sell my people to Government.

15. I shall never help the missionaries in their Christian faith to ruin our traditional and cultural customs. . . .

17. I shall never steal any property belonging to a member of our society.

18. I shall obey any strike call, whenever notified. . . .

21. I shall always follow the leadership of Jomo Kenyatta and Mbiyu Koinange.'

* *Kikuyu Central Association*

From Donald L. Barnett and Karari Njama, *Mau Mau From Within*, Macgibbon and Kee, 1966.

---

1 What do you think was the purpose of the ritual performed before the oath was administered?

2 Judging by points 1 to 6 of the oath, what kind of organisation was Mau Mau?

3 Using points 7 to 21 of the oath, describe in your own words the aims of Mau Mau.

In the ferocious Mau Mau rising of 1952–59 some 11,000 Kikuyu were killed, often brutally, by both the British security forces and by Mau Mau. 80,000 people were imprisoned in concentration camps. By 1959 the British government had realised that it was impossible to crush the desire of Kenyans for independence by using force. Bowing to the inevitable, it granted Kenyans the right of self-government in 1963, and Kenya became an independent republic with Jomo Kenyatta as President in 1964.

Kenya was not the only African territory to experience the forces of nationalism in the 1950s. In the Gold Coast (now Ghana) another of the delegates at the 1945 Pan-African Congress, Kwame Nkrumah, built up a mass nationalist movement, gaining independence for Ghana in 1957. Similar movements were active in every other European-controlled territory. By 1960, the British government had decided to abandon the policy outlined in source B. Harold Macmillan, the

British Prime Minister, explained the new approach of his government in a speech to the South African parliament on 3 February 1960:

E In the twentieth century and especially since the end of the war the processes which gave birth to the nation states of Europe have been repeated all over the world. We have seen the awakening of national consciousness in peoples who have for centuries lived in dependence on some other power. Fifteen years ago this movement spread through Asia. Many countries there of different races and civilisations pressed their claim to an independent life. Today the same thing is happening in Africa and the most striking of all the impressions I have formed since leaving London is of the strength of this African national consciousness. In different places it takes different forms, but it is happening everywhere. The wind of change is blowing through this continent, and whether we like it or not this growth of national consciousness is a political fact, and our national policies must take account of it.

Quoted in T. Walter Wallbank, *Contemporary Africa, Continent in Transition*, Van Nostrand, 1964.

1 What do you think Macmillan meant by 'national consciousness'?
2 How does he suggest that the growth of national consciousness in Africa was unstoppable?

As Macmillan said, the wind of change was blowing through the whole of Africa, not just the British-controlled part of it. By the end of 1960, nineteen African states had gained their independence, with more shortly to follow. And in some of those states the wind of change blew at hurricane force, bringing with it not only independence but also a host of new problems. One such state was the Congo (now Zaire) from which the Belgians withdrew in 1960. In a speech at the Independence Day celebrations, the new Prime Minister, Patrice Lumumba, had this to say to the departing Belgians:

F No Congolese worthy of that name will ever forget that independence has been won by struggle. . . .

Our lot was eighty years of colonial rule; our wounds are still too fresh and painful to be driven from our memory.

We have known tiring labour exacted in exchange for salary which did not allow us to satisfy our hunger, to clothe and lodge ourselves decently or raise our children like loved beings.

We have known ironies, insults, blows which we had to endure morning, noon and night because we were 'Negroes.'. . .

We have known that the law was never the same depending on whether it concerned a white or a Negro: accommodating for one group, it was cruel and inhuman for the other.

We have known the atrocious sufferings of those banished for political opinions or religious beliefs. . . .

We have known there were magnificent houses for the whites in the cities and tumble-down straw huts for the Negroes, that a Negro was not admitted in movie-houses or restaurants, or stores labelled

'European', that a Negro travelled in the hulls of river boats at the feet of the white in his first class cabin.

All that, my brothers, we have profoundly suffered. . . .

From T. Walter Wallbank, *Documents on Modern Africa*, Van Nostrand, 1964.

---

1 According to source F, in what ways did Africans in the Congo suffer under Belgian rule? To what extent is this confirmed by source F in chapter 1 (page 4)?
2 How reliable do you consider source F as evidence of how the Belgians ruled the Congo before 1960? Explain your answer.

The 'profound suffering' of the Congolese people continued even after they had gained independence. As soon as the Belgian army left the country, a confused and ugly conflict for power broke out, disfiguring the Congo for the next five years, with the army seizing control in 1965.

Other newly-independent African states showed a similar tendency to fight wars and to fall under military rule. By 1975, half the forty-one independent states in Africa were ruled by military governments; and among and between themselves, they had fought some thirty civil and foreign wars.

The wars and military coups of the African states in their first twenty years of independence led many old European colonialists to look back fondly on the days when they, rather than Africans, ruled the 'Dark Continent'. One of them, Sir James Robertson, a colonial administrator in the Sudan Political Service, said in a radio interview in 1979:

G I think a great deal is now spoken by people who don't know very much about the background to our rule in Africa. When we took over many of these countries there was very little government, there was very little civilisation, there was a great deal of inter-tribal warfare. Our policy in these countries was, as Virgil said, *imponere paces mores*, to impose the ways of peace, and that's what we did, and we developed them as best we could. One of the things our critics seem to forget is that we had no money. The British government gave us nothing for many, many years. In Sudan, which I know best, when Kitchener defeated the armies of the Mahdi at Omdurman in 1898 there were no railways, there were no telegraphs, there were no schools, there were no hospitals, there was no sort of modern government with ministries or anything of that kind. And when we left the Sudan [in 1955] there was a system of railways, there was a system of roads, there was a police force, there was an army, there were hospitals, there were schools, there was even a university. This was all done in the space of about fifty-eight years – and you could walk from one end of the Sudan to the other more safely than you could walk in the back streets of London, without any fear of danger. We had set up a civilisation which had not existed before.

From Charles Allen (ed.), *Tales From the Dark Continent*, André Deutsch/BBC, 1979.

1 Judging by what he says in source G, what did Sir James Robertson mean by 'civilisation'?
2 Suggest how critics of the European colonies, such as the Pan-African Congress (source A), Jomo Kenyatta (source C), members of Mau Mau (source D) or Patrice Lumumba (source F), might argue against Sir James Robertson's point of view.

In the deep south of the African continent, one state defied the trend of the 1960s and 1970s towards black African independence. This was the Republic of South Africa, which has used a system of 'apartheid' to prevent its non-white citizens from gaining independence. Introduced as law in 1948, apartheid means segregating people according to the colour of their skins. Where people live and work depends largely on whether they are 'black', 'coloured', 'Indian' or 'white'. This classification of 'race' is also used to segregate public amenities such as trains, buses and taxis, hospitals, libraries, museums, toilets, cinemas, theatres, hotels, clubs and beaches. Source H, a photograph taken on a South African beach in 1969, illustrates this:

H

How has the South African government justified the policy of apartheid? A typical argument in favour of white supremacy can be seen in source I, taken from the State of South Africa Yearbook, a government publication of 1963:

1. In one respect South Africa's policy differs radically from that in the rest of Africa. South Africa has never been exclusively a Black man's country. The Bantu have no greater claim to it than its white population. Bantu tribes from Central and East Africa invaded South Africa at the time when Europeans landed at the Cape. . . .

2. The areas chosen by the Bantu 300 years ago are still in Bantu hands and they have been made inalienable Bantu Areas by the South African government in 1913. By setting aside these areas for the exclusive use of the Bantu, the Government was guided by the desire to create national homelands for the larger national units of the Bantu. These homelands will form the nuclei of self-governing Bantu states.

3. The South African Government has accepted the desire of Colonial people for self-rule as a natural right. . . . South Africa has its dependent people within her own borders. The granting of independence can, therefore, not follow the political pattern worked out by the colonial powers of Europe. . . .

6. It is well nigh impossible to create one nation out of the different population groups inhabiting the Republic of South Africa. Each group clings to its own culture, language and traditions. This natural trend must be respected. . . .

8. Western democracy is foreign to Bantu tradition. All over Africa the tendency is towards a one-party state under a Black dictator. To adopt the principle of One Man-One Vote in South Africa would hand over the culturally advanced groups, i.e. the Whites, Coloureds and Indians, to the mercies of a Bantu leader who might well have Communistic affiliations.

From The State of South Africa, *Yearbook*, 1963.

---

1 According to source I, why does the South African government not allow black people the right of self-rule?

2 What do sources H and I tell you about the nature of white rule in South Africa?

The policy mentioned in point 2 of source I, that of creating self-governing 'homelands' for black people, eventually gave 13 per cent of South Africa to its black population. The lands which they received, officially called 'black national states', can be seen on the next page in source J, a map produced in Britain in 1985.

J

Source: *The Times*, 3 April 1985.

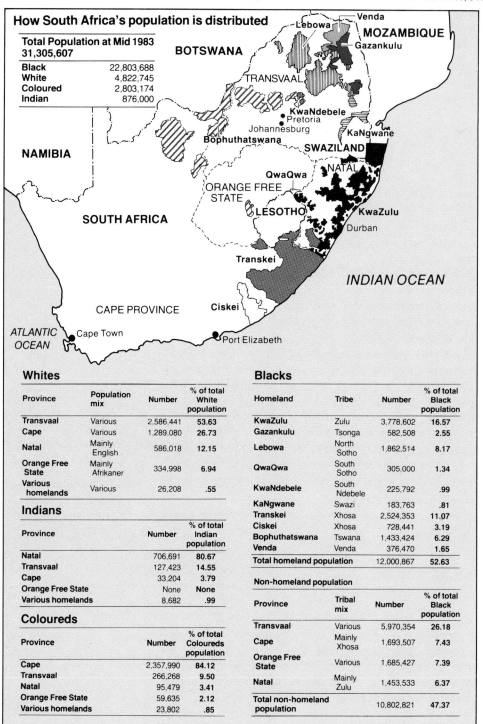

How South Africa's population is distributed

Total Population at Mid 1983
31,305,607

Black	22,803,688
White	4,822,745
Coloured	2,803,174
Indian	876,000

Whites

Province	Population mix	Number	% of total White population
Transvaal	Various	2,586,441	53.63
Cape	Various	1,289,080	26.73
Natal	Mainly English	586,018	12.15
Orange Free State	Mainly Afrikaner	334,998	6.94
Various homelands	Various	26,208	.55

Indians

Province	Number	% of total Indian population
Natal	706,691	80.67
Transvaal	127,423	14.55
Cape	33,204	3.79
Orange Free State	None	None
Various homelands	8,682	.99

Coloureds

Province	Number	% of total Coloureds population
Cape	2,357,990	84.12
Transvaal	266,268	9.50
Natal	95,479	3.41
Orange Free State	59,635	2.12
Various homelands	23,802	.85

Blacks

Homeland	Tribe	Number	% of total Black population
KwaZulu	Zulu	3,778,602	16.57
Gazankulu	Tsonga	582,508	2.55
Lebowa	North Sotho	1,862,514	8.17
QwaQwa	South Sotho	305,000	1.34
KwaNdebele	South Ndebele	225,792	.99
KaNgwane	Swazi	183,763	.81
Transkei	Xhosa	2,524,353	11.07
Ciskei	Xhosa	728,441	3.19
Bophuthatswana	Tswana	1,433,424	6.29
Venda	Venda	376,470	1.65
Total homeland population		**12,000,867**	**52.63**

Non-homeland population

Province	Tribal mix	Number	% of total Black population
Transvaal	Various	5,970,354	26.18
Cape	Mainly Xhosa	1,693,507	7.43
Orange Free State	Various	1,685,427	7.39
Natal	Mainly Zulu	1,453,533	6.37
Total non-homeland population		**10,802,821**	**47.37**

---

1 Using the information in source J, list the ways in which the 'black national states', or 'homelands', differ from the rest of South Africa. You should consider such factors as (a) size, (b) location, (c) population density, (d) economic viability, (e) trade opportunities.

Black Africans have opposed apartheid in many ways since its introduction in 1948. Although it is a criminal offence to belong to it, the African National Congress has become the largest black nationalist organisation in South Africa, using a variety of tactics to fight apartheid. Among the tactics that the ANC adopted in the 1960s were strikes, civil disobedience and sabotage. Nelson Mandela, the best-known leader of the ANC, explained why they were prepared to use violence in a speech at his trial for sabotage in 1964:

K I planned sabotage as a result of many years of tyranny, exploitation and oppression of my people by the whites. Fifty years of non-violence had brought the African people even fewer rights. We fight against poverty and loss of human dignity. Africans want to be paid a living wage. Africans want to perform work which they are capable of doing and not work which the government declare them capable of. We want to be allowed to live where we obtain work and not to be endorsed out of an area because we were not born there. We want to be allowed to own places where we work. . . . African men want to have their wives and children to live with them where they work and not be forced into an unnatural existence in men's hostels. Our women want to be with their menfolk and not to be left permanently widowed in the reserves. We want to be allowed out after 11 o'clock at night and not to be confined to our rooms like little children. We want a just share in the whole of South Africa.

Above all we want political rights.

Our struggle is a truly national one. It is a struggle of the African people inspired by our own suffering and our own experience. It is a struggle for the right to live.

Quoted in Mary Benson, *South Africa: The Struggle for a Birthright*, Penguin, 1966.

1 What does this speech tell you about the conditions of life for black people in the 'homelands'?
2 How does Mandela justify the use of violence in the struggle against apartheid?

Using sources A to K in this chapter, as well as sources B, C, E, F and I in chapter 1:
1 make a list of reasons why Africans wanted independence from European rule;
2 which of these reasons appear to have been the most important?

13 The jewel in the crown? India, 1900–47

At the start of the twentieth century India was, in Queen Victoria's words, 'the jewel in the crown' of the British Empire – the richest and most glamorous of Britain's many overseas territories. The British had been in India for two hundred years, and their authority was firmly established. Around a thousand senior officials of the Indian Civil Service ran the affairs of 350 million people, while a Viceroy with almost unlimited powers had final authority over their every affair, great and small. And at the summit of the British 'Raj' was the British monarch, to whom – in British eyes – all Indians owed loyalty and obedience.

The remarkable nature of British rule in India is reflected in the diary of King George V on 12 December 1911. It describes the Delhi Durbar, a ceremonial court held by King George and Queen Mary as Emperor and Empress of India, in the ancient Moghul city of Delhi:

A Today we held the Coronation Durbar, the most beautiful and wonderful sight I ever saw, & one which I shall never forget. . . .

The weather was all that could be wished, hot sun, hardly any wind, no clouds. May* & I were photographed before we started in our robes, I wore the same clothes and robes as at the Coronation with a new crown made for India which cost £60,000 which the Indian government is going to pay for. . . . The Amphitheatre contained about 12,000 people, there were some 18,000 troops inside it & over 50,000 people on the Mound. On our arrival we took our seats on the thrones facing the centre of the crescent. I first made a speech giving the reasons for holding the Durbar. Then the Governor General did homage to me followed by all the Ruling Chiefs, Governors, Lieut.-Governors and members of the different Councils. We then walked in procession, I holding May's hand, our trains being held by young Maharajahs* . . . to two other silver thrones raised up on a platform facing the troops & the Mound. . . . Then all the troops presented arms & a salute of 101 Guns was fired & a feu de joi*. . . . We returned in procession to the first thrones when I announced that the Capital will be transferred from Calcutta to Delhi, the ancient capital. . . .

The whole of the people present then sung the National Anthem & the most wonderful Durbar ever held was closed. . . .

Reached the Camp at 3.0. Rather tired after wearing my crown for $3\frac{1}{2}$ hours, it hurt my head, as it is pretty heavy. . . .

Afterwards we held a reception in the large tent, about 5,000 people came, the heat was simply awful. Bed at 11.0 & quite tired.

* *Queen Mary*

* *Indian princes*

* *running fire of guns*

Quoted in John Gore, *King George V: a Personal Memoir*, John Murray, 1941.

---

1 Judging by this account, what were the purposes of the Delhi Durbar?
2 Why do you think the Indian government was prepared to pay £60,000 (approx. £1.5 million in 1989 values) for 'a new crown made for India'?

The pomp and circumstance of rituals like the Delhi Durbar disguised the fact that many Indians wanted an end to British rule. Since 1885 an Indian National Congress had been pressing for the right of self-government and for a greater measure of equality for Indians. As one Congress member said in a speech in 1897:

B Just look for a moment at the training we are receiving. From our earliest schooldays the great English writers have been our classics. Englishmen have been our professors. . . . English history is taught in our schools. The books we generally read are English books. . . . It is impossible not to be penetrated by English ideas, not to acquire English concepts of duty, of rights, of brotherhood. . . . Imbued with these ideas and principles, we naturally desire to acquire the full rights and to share the responsibilities of British citizenship.

Quoted by Michael Edwardes, 'Revolt Against the Raj', in *The British Empire*, Time-Life Books, 1972.

1 What kind of person do you think made this speech?
2 To what kind of people does he/she appear to be speaking?

By the end of the First World War, 1914–18, in which 62,000 Indian soldiers had died, Indian nationalists were much louder in their demands for self-government and national independence. The hardships of the war, and an influenza epidemic which killed 16 million Indians by its end, caused widespread discontent. Although the Montagu-Chelmsford reforms of 1919 introduced a form of power-sharing between the British and Indians, there were still many reasons why Indians disliked British rule. The most important of these was the behaviour of the British army at Amritsar in April 1919. It is described in source C by Michael Edwardes, a British historian writing in 1972:

C Amritsar was a holy city, the centre of the faith of the Sikhs. . . . two nationalist leaders were arrested and a large crowd tried to enter the area of the city occupied by Europeans. They were turned back by armed police and began rioting, firing buildings and murdering Europeans in the very centre of the city instead.

The next day, Brigadier-General Reginald Dyer, an Irishman born and educated in India, arrived in Amritsar. His first act was to prohibit all public meetings. . . . At one o'clock on that day, Dyer was told that a public meeting had been called for half-past four on a large piece of waste land known as the Jallianwala Bagh. . . .

The area was roughly a square, quite large, and almost completely surrounded by houses. Four narrow entrances, wide enough to let three or four people walk abreast, led into the Bagh from the surrounding streets. Dyer decided to wait and then, when the meeting had begun, make an example of those who had defied his orders. By four o'clock he heard that a great crowd had gathered in the Bagh – perhaps 5,000, perhaps as many as 25,000. His informants were not precise. . . . Apparently, Dyer's intention was to disperse the crowd by firing over their heads and speeding them on their way by driving his armoured cars through what he obviously believed to be an open space. He did not expect much trouble, for he took only 90 men with him to deal with the meeting.

When Dyer arrived at the Bagh he discovered that his armoured cars could not get through the narrow entrances. Moving with his men into the Bagh itself he was faced with a vast crowd, being harangued by speakers who were, he was convinced – though he could not hear them – rousing the mob to violence. There is little doubt that Dyer panicked, but he did not do the sensible thing and retire. Instead, he ordered his men to fire, without warning, into the crowd until their ammunition was exhausted. On his own admission, 1,605 rounds were fired. It was the crowd's turn to panic. As men tried to climb the walls they were picked off by gunfire, children ran screaming, some women threw themselves down a well. It was all over in ten minutes. Dyer withdrew, ordering the entrances to be blocked so that no one could escape and no medical attention reach the wounded. Officially, 379 were killed and over 1,560 wounded. Unofficially there were probably a great many more.

Dyer went away thinking that his action had saved the Punjab from anarchy. But he had not restored order in Amritsar. Two days later he declared martial law, which was not lifted until June 9. During that period, anyone passing through the street where a woman missionary had been brutally attacked was forced to crawl on all fours; refusal meant being whipped. Public floggings were imposed for such minor offences as 'the contravention of the curfew order, failure to salaam to a commissioned officer, for disrespect to a European, or refusal to sell milk.' . . .

From Michael Edwardes, 'Revolt Against the Raj', in *The British Empire*, Time-Life Books, 1972.

---

1 According to source C, why did General Dyer order the crowd to disperse?

2 What impression does the writer create of (a) Dyer, and (b) the nature of British rule in India?

Many people believed that General Dyer had acted correctly at Amritsar. Their view is reflected in source D, a poster produced in 1920 after a committee of enquiry into the Amritsar Massacre criticised Dyer's actions, and forced him to retire from the army.

D

DYER APPRECIATION FUND
An appeal for funds to present GENERAL DYER with A Sword of Honour and a Purse, is hereby made to all well-wishers of India, both European and Indian,
AS A MARK OF
GRATITUDE to General Dyer for sparing India untold misery by arresting murder and wholesale anarchy.
SYMPATHY with him for the unjust sentence passed on him
Sympathisers are requested to form local committees all over India to further the cause.
Subscriptions should be sent to the President, Dyer Appreciation Fund, Mussoorie, or branches of the Allahbad and Alliance Banks, Ltd

---

1 Why, according to this poster, did some people support General Dyer's actions at Amritsar in 1919?
2 From the viewpoint of an Indian nationalist, explain why you would not contribute to the 'Dyer Appreciation Fund'.

The horro   Amritsar Massacre led many uncommitted Indians to join the   ss Party, now led by Mohandas Gandhi, a small, sweet-nature   skilful lawyer-politician. Gandhi responded to British brutalit   new and surprising method of political warfare, civil disobedien   ce E shows one of the many forms that civil disobedience co   it is a poster issued by the Congress Party calling for a hartal   strike. in protest against a visit to India in 1921 by George V's son,   the Prince of Wales.

E

From a private collection.

1 Describe in your own words the kind of protest called for f   is poster.
2 What do you think the organisers hoped to achieve with this kind of protest?

Another form of protest involved the use of what Gandhi called 'satya-graha', or 'soul force'. This meant non-violent resistance to British rule: it meant, in Gandhi's words, 'the conquest of an adversary by suffering in one's own person'. In many cases, Gandhi's followers did not fully grasp what 'soul force' meant, so throughout the 1920s and 1930s, their non-violent protests often erupted into rioting and bloodshed. The problem is reflected in this British cartoon of 1930.

F

Source: *Punch*

A FRANKENSTEIN OF THE EAST.

GANDHI. "REMEMBER—NO VIOLENCE; JUST DISOBEDIENCE."
GENIE. "AND WHAT IF I DISOBEY *YOU?*"

1 Explain the point you think the cartoonist was trying to make.
2 Do you think the cartoonist was sympathetic or hostile to Gandhi? Explain your answer.

Some of the difficulties involved in using 'satyagraha' can be seen in source G. It was written in May 1930 by an American press corre-spondent who saw what happened when Gandhi's followers tried to raid a salt-making plant in violation of British law regarding the manufacture and sale of salt.

G 'Suddenly at a word of command, scores of native policemen rushed upon the advancing marchers and rained blows on their heads with their steel-shod lathis*. Not one of the marchers even raised an arm to fend off the blows. They went down like ten-pins. From where I stood I heard that sickening whack of the clubs on unprotected skulls. The waiting crowd of marchers groaned and sucked in their breath in sympathetic pain at every blow. . . . They marched steadily, with heads up, without the encouragement of music or cheering or any possibility that they might escape serious injury or death. The police rushed out and methodically beat down the second column. There was no fight, no struggle; the marchers simply walked forward till struck down.'

* clubs

Quoted in Ved Mehta, *Mahatma Gandhi and His Apostles*, Penguin Books, 1976.

---

1 How can you explain the behaviour of (a) the marchers, and (b) the policemen?
2 What light does source G shed on the nature of British rule in India in 1930?

During the 1930s the British slowly and reluctantly came to realise that their days in India were numbered. The British Parliament showed that it realised this by passing the Government of India Act in 1935, giving Indians a much greater share of political authority. But as the harshness of British rule began to diminish, a new and dangerous problem came to the forefront of Indian politics: a deep division between Muslims and Hindus in the Congress Party over the future structure of an independent Indian nation. Mohammed Ali Jinnah, leader of the Muslim League, which demanded the creation of a separate 'Pakistan' for Indian Muslims, described some of the things that separated Muslims from Hindus in an interview in 1944:

H How can you even dream of Hindu-Muslim unity? Everything pulls us apart. We have no inter-marriages. We have not the same calendar. The Muslims believe in a single God, and the Hindus are idolatrous. Like the Christians, the Muslims believe in an egalitarian society, whereas the Hindus maintain the iniquitous system of castes and leave heartlessly fifty million untouchables to their fate, at the bottom of the social ladder. Now again, the Hindus worship animals. They consider cows sacred. We, the Muslims, think it is nonsense. We want to kill the cows. We want to eat them. Another thing: no Hindu will take food from a Muslim. . . . Indeed, when you look into the problem, you see that there are only two links between the Muslims and the Hindus: British rule – and the common desire to get rid of it.

From Eve Curie, *Journey Among Warriors*, Heinemann, 1943.

---

1 Explain in your own words why Jinnah thought that unity between India's Hindus and Muslims was impossible.

The chasm between Hindus and Muslims was not the only difficulty facing those who wanted to make India an independent nation. Some other difficulties are described by a British historian writing in 1985:

I   Who spoke for India?... Could anyone speak for India? In 1945 India was over 400 million people: 250 million Hindus, 90 million Muslims, 6 million Sikhs, millions of sectarians, Buddhists, Christians; 500 independent princes and maharajahs; 23 main languages, 200 dialects; 3000 castes, with 60 million 'untouchables' at the bottom of the heap; 80 per cent of the nation lived in 500,000 villages, most of them inaccessible, even by surfaced road.

From Paul Johnson, *A History of the Modern World, from 1917 to the 1980s*, Weidenfeld and Nicolson, 1985.

As soon as the independent states of India and Pakistan came into being in 1947, fourteen million Hindus, Muslims and Sikhs left their homes and fled towards 'their' side of the new frontiers. In many places one lot of refugees massacred another moving in the opposite direction. For nine months after Independence Day, roadsides were littered with the mutilated corpses of tortured men, women and children. Entire trainloads of butchered corpses steamed into Lahore and Delhi each week. The worst violence took place in the Punjab, whose territory straddled the new nations. Some idea of the appalling scale of violence can be gained from the newspaper report in source J.

J
                                    September 1, 1947
                        From Douglas Brown, Daily Telegraph
                                    Special Correspondent
                                          LAHORE
An average guess at the number of victims in the Punjab civil war, computed on the basis of such facts as are definitely known, gives the figures of 100,000 dead and 300,000 homeless.

The present state of public order in Lahore is exemplified by the fate of six Sikhs acquitted of murder by the District Court. All were stabbed to death before they left the precincts, one while sheltering behind the judge's chair.

The waylaying of express trains to murder members of one or the other community has become almost a matter of routine.

Little by little, Muslim troops will leave India (Hindustan) and Sikh and Hindu troops Pakistan, except for the actual function of protecting and escorting refugees. The responsibility for law and order will then rest squarely on the two Governments concerned.

A minority community I visited today have no faith whatever in the new arrangements and await extermination in a spirit of tragic fatalism. They are the Sikhs of Nankana Sahib, 40 miles inside Pakistan.

If Amritsar is the Rome of Sikhism, Nankana Sahib is its Bethlehem. The founder of Sikhism, Guru Nanak, was born there in the fifteenth century. Sikhs have been evacuating their villages all round, but at Nankana Sahib they stay.

I spoke to Sirdar Narain Singh, the blue-turbanned guardian of the chief temple, the head of this community of 5,000 people now swollen to 20,000 by refugees. He said:

'The ring is closing round us. Five miles away Sikh villages are at the mercy of Muslims. We expect an attack here at any moment.'

All Sikhs by religious precept carry swords. A British major stationed at Nankana Sahib believes that they have many more arms stowed away in their multitudinous temples. There is no doubt they will fight.

On the way back, travelling with a British brigadier in a jeep through the flooded countryside, we met whole posses of Muslims, armed with spears, closing in on Nankana Sahib. The brigadier, who has 2,000 troops with seven British officers to control a population of a million, had no means of dispersing the bands.

From *The Daily Telegraph*, 1 September 1947.

K New Delhi station in September 1947: refugees cram a train bound for Pakistan

1 Why did the people of Nankana Sahib not flee from the town?

2 Why do you think the people of Nankana Sahib had no faith in the new arrangements for maintaining law and order in India and Pakistan?

3 Judging by source J, why was the death toll in the Punjab so high?

4 In source K, what do you think was the religion of the refugees? Where do you think they hoped to go on the train, and why do you think so many attempted to travel on that train?

1 Using sources A to E in this chapter as evidence, describe the features of British rule which Indian nationalist leaders most disliked.

2 Using sources F to K as evidence, explain why the movement for Indian independence involved a great deal of bloodshed and violence.

14 A thirty-year war: Indo-China, 1945–75

Until 1945 the French colonies in Indo-China (now called Vietnam, Laos and Kampuchea) did not figure greatly in international affairs. Throughout the Second World War, when Indo-China was occupied by the Japanese, neither the Allied nor the Axis leaders gave much thought to its long-term future. But when, in September 1945, a Communist independence movement called the Vietminh proclaimed a Vietnamese Republic under the leadership of Ho Chi Minh, Indo-China became for the first time an object of international concern. The French, who intended to re-establish their control of Indo-China after the defeat of Japan, were not prepared to accept Vietnamese independence. Nor were the British or the Chinese, whose troops occupied Indo-China from 1945–46 to supervise the withdrawal of the defeated Japanese. The scene was therefore set for a struggle to decide the political future of the peoples of Indo-China. It was a struggle that would last, on and off, for thirty years, killing some two million people, destroying vast tracts of the country, and leaving countless millions homeless and bereaved.

The thirty-year war in Indo-China began as a colonial struggle of Vietnamese Communists against the French. Some of the issues at stake in that struggle were described by Ho Chi Minh, leader of the Vietminh, in a speech in 1945:

A For over eighty years the gang of French colonialists, operating under the three colours which are supposed to stand for liberty, equality and fraternity, have stolen our land and oppressed our people. . . . The French have not given us political freedom, they have instituted a barbarous legal code, they have opened more prisons than schools, they have drowned all our attempts at revolt in rivers of blood, they have sought to besot our race with opium and alcohol. . . . In the economic sphere they have stripped us to the bone, they have stolen our paddy fields, our estates, our forests, our mines.

So we, the Provisional Government of the new Vietnam, the representatives of the people, declare that we repudiate the French colonialist regime . . . the treaties signed between France and our own country and all the privileges which the French claim over our country. . . . The people are of one heart in affirming their determination to fight the French colonialists.

Quoted in Jean Lacoutre, *Ho Chi Minh* (translated by P. Wiles), Allen Lane, 1969.

---

1 Explain in your own words what you think Ho Chi Minh meant by 'the three colours which are supposed to stand for liberty, equality and fraternity'.
2 Why, according to this speech, did Ho Chi Minh reject 'the French colonialist regime'? Which of those reasons seems to have been the most important in his eyes? Explain your answer.

The ensuing war between the French and the Vietminh lasted for more than seven years and killed an estimated 600,000 people on both sides. It is unlikely that the war could have lasted so long if the French had not received help from the United States. By 1954 the United States government had poured $1.4 billion into the French war effort. Richard Nixon, Vice-President of the United States, explained why his country was doing so in a speech in December 1953:

B Why is the United States spending hundreds of millions of dollars supporting the forces of the French Union in the fight against Communism? If Indo-China falls, Thailand is put in an almost impossible position. The same is true of Malaya with its rubber and tin. The same is true of Indonesia. If this whole part of South-East Asia goes under Communist domination or Communist influence, Japan, who trades and must trade with this area in order to exist, must inevitably be oriented towards the Communist regime.

From Allan B. Cole (ed.), *Conflict in Indo-China and International Repercussions: A Documentary History 1945–55*, Cornell University Press, 1956.

---

1 In your own words, explain why the United States gave military aid to the French in Indo-China.

After the withdrawal of French forces from Indo-China in 1954, the United States government gave aid directly to the newly-created state of South Vietnam, and began training a South Vietnamese army. When an anti-Communist Catholic politician, Ngo Dinh Diem, became the first President of South Vietnam after rigged elections in 1955, the United States gave him its full support, with economic aid totalling $3,000 million over the next four years.

President Diem governed South Vietnam as a dictator, imprisoning and executing political opponents and persecuting Buddhists, the country's dominant religious group. In 1963, however, Diem's Buddhist opponents helped to bring about his overthrow when they staged a series of dramatic protests against him. Source C shows the first of those protests – the suicide by fire of Thich Quang Duc, a Buddhist priest, in Saigon on 11 June 1963. Largely as a result of the suicide campaign, in which eleven Buddhists burned themselves to death, the United States government cut off aid to Diem and helped his generals to murder him in a coup in November 1963.

C

Malcolm Browne, the photographer who took those pictures, later wrote that:

D The pictures I took of the death of Thich Quang Duc came to have an existence of their own as they circulated around the world. They meant many things to many people. . . .

A group of prominent American clergymen used one of the pictures as the basis for full page advertisements in the New York Times and Washington Post, over the heading: 'We, too, protest'. Their protest was aimed against American support of the Diem regime.

Communist China reportedly printed millions of copies of one of the pictures for distribution throughout Asia and Africa. These pictures were captioned 'A Buddhist monk gives his life in the struggle against US/Diem imperialism.' . . .

In a conference with US Ambassador Frederick E. Nolting, Jr., President Diem asked if it were true that I had bribed the monks to set up the suicide so as to get an eye-catching picture.

From Malcolm W. Browne, *The New Face of War: A Report on a Communist Guerilla Campaign*, Cassell, 1965.

---

1 Study sources C and D. Suggest why the photographs had such a great effect on public opinion around the world.
2 Do you think that Thich Quang Duc's suicide would have been any less effective as a protest if no photographer had been present? Explain your answer.
3 How can sources C and D be used as evidence of the strength of feeling against President Diem's regime?

The world's press played a crucial part in shaping public opinion about the war in Indo-China. Film crews and cameramen, journalists and reporters covered the war more thoroughly than any previous war, and helped to bring into existence a powerful anti-war protest movement at the end of the 1960s. Sources E and F illustrate two of the ways in which the press could influence public opinion about the war.

E From the *Akron (Ohio) Beacon Journal* Monday, 27 March 1967
To the Editor:
Here are portions of a letter I have received from my son, who is now stationed in Vietnam. My son enlisted in the Army, asked to be sent to Vietnam and backed the government's strong policy towards the war in Vietnam – at least he did so when he left this country last November. I believe what he has to say will be of interest to you and your readers.
'Dear Mom and Dad:
Today we went on a mission and I'm not very proud of myself, my friends or my country. We burned every hut in sight!

It was a small rural network of villages and the people were incredibly poor. My unit burned and plundered their meagre possessions. Let me try to explain the situation to you.

The huts here are thatched palm leaves. Each one has a dried mud bunker inside. These bunkers are to protect the families. Kind of like air-raid shelters.

My unit commanders, however, chose to think that these bunkers are offensive. So every hut we find that has a bunker, we are ordered to burn to the ground!

When the ten helicopters landed this morning, in the midst of these huts, and six men jumped out of each "chopper", we were firing the moment we hit the ground. We fired into all the huts we could. Then we got "on line" and swept the area.

It is then that we burn these huts and take all men old enough to carry a weapon and the "choppers" come and get them (they take them to a collection point a few miles away for interrogation.) The

Vietcong fill their minds with tales saying the GIs* kill all their men.   * *American soldiers*

So, everyone is crying, begging and praying that we don't separate them and take their husbands, sons and grandfathers. The women wail and moan.

Then they watch in terror as we burn their homes, personal possessions and food. Yes, we burn all rice and shoot all livestock.

Some of the guys are so careless! Today a buddy of mine called "La Dai" ("Come here") into a hut and an old man came out of the bomb shelter. My buddy told the old man to get away from the hut . . . and threw a hand grenade into the shelter.

As he pulled the pin the old man got excited and started jabbering and running towards my buddy and the hut. A GI, not understanding, stopped the old man with a football tackle just as my buddy threw the grenade into the shelter. (There is a four-second delay on a hand grenade.)

After he threw it, and was running for cover (during this four second delay) we all heard a baby crying from inside the shelter.

There was nothing we could do . . .

After the explosion we found the mother, two children (ages about six and twelve, boy and girl) and an almost newborn baby. That is what the old man was trying to tell us! . . .

IT WAS HORRIBLE!!

The children's fragile bodies were torn apart, literally mutilated. We looked at each other and burned the hut . . .

Well, Dad, you wanted to know what it's like here. Does this give you an idea? . . .

Your Son.'

The rest of my son's letter goes on to describe what the routines of his life in Vietnam are like. He described an uneventful ambush he participated in, and he got excited about a new-type rifle he had been issued. Beyond that, there are personal matters which he discussed.

Needless to say, I was very much disturbed to read this´ letter . . .

I have not been a dove as far as the Vietnamese war is concerned, though I have not been a strong hawk either. But I think the American people should understand what they mean when they advocate a continuation and even an escalation of our war effort in Vietnam.

A GI's DAD

From John Gerassi, *North Vietnam: A Documentary*, Allen and Unwin, 1968.

---

1 Judging by the son's letter, what were the military purposes of the mission he describes?

2 What do you think the GI's Dad hoped to achieve by sending his son's letter to a newspaper?

3 What might a supporter of America's war effort in Vietnam have said in response to this letter?

4 What uses can a historian make of this material? What problems might there be in using the material for historical purposes?

Source F is a photograph taken in South Vietnam in 1967 by an American photographer, Dana Stone. It shows a father cradling his dead son in his arms after members of the United States First Cavalry fought a battle against the Viet Cong in his village.

F

1 What do you think the photographer was hoping to achieve by taking this photograph?

2 Suggest why so many newspaper and magazine editors published it.

3 Can you tell from the photograph what the opinions of the photographer about the Vietnam War might have been? Explain your answer.

The end of the Vietnam War in 1975 did not bring peace to all of Indo-China. In Cambodia, the Communist Khmer Rouge took power in April 1975. Led by Pol Pot, they drove the three million inhabitants of the capital, Phnom Penh, into the countryside, and set about creating an entirely new kind of society, based on forced labour communes known as New Villages. The New Villages were described in 1976 by two American journalists, John Barron and Anthony Paul, in their book *Peace with Horror*. They gained their information from interviews with thirty-three villagers who managed to escape into neighbouring Thailand:

G Ampil Pram Daum . . . once was a large village in the midst of fertile rice fields. The original residents had disappeared, and their vacant houses, though damaged and decaying, could have provided shelter for many of the approximately 2000 refugees Angka Loeu* had consigned to the locale. However, consistent with its determination to wipe away the past entirely and start society anew, Angka Loeu prohibited anyone from living in the old village. All had to build their own huts on the edge of the forest and create a completely New Village.

* 'The Higher Organisation' – the Communists

Characteristically, a New Village at birth consisted of little except a designated area of land, the people shanghaied to develop it and Angka supervisors. Angka allotted each arriving family a space, usually about five metres square, on which to build a hut. Normally, neither materials nor tools were provided, so the family had to forage for bamboo, branches, palm leaves, straw, grass, or whatever else useful the forest and jungles might yield. . . .

Upon completion of the hut family members joined the common labor force engaged in clearing trees and underbrush, plowing for the planting of rice and erection of irrigation dikes. Children under six, women in the last stages of pregnancy, the very aged and, generally but not always, the extremely ill were exempted from work. Otherwise, having been awakened by a gong, everybody labored from 5.30 or 6.00 a.m. to 11 a.m. and 1 or 2 to 5 p.m. seven days a week, irrespective of rain or heat. In some settlements work resumed for three hours at night if the moon was out. Men, women and children were segregated into separate work parties and kept apart in the fields. Except during the midday break, Angka guards allowed neither rest nor conversation during work. . . .

In the evenings, unless fieldwork was required under the moon-light, Angka Loeu compelled all New Villagers throughout Cambodia to attend ideological lectures that droned on for three or four hours. . . . Frequently, the assembled also witnessed one of the gravest of village events, a ceremony known as a Kosang, the Khmer word for 'construction'. A Kosang was a formal and ritualistic warning to someone who had displeased Angka Loeu. The transgressor was expected to submit to public humiliation, then to 'construct' himself or herself into a good and pure person by confessing and repenting the sin alleged. Always a Kosang evoked fear and silence among the onlookers, for everyone quickly learned that no one ever received more than two Kosangs ...

Kosangs were followed by revolutionary education, during which speakers by rote repeated ... 'You must forget everything you have learned ... You must learn to hate the former regime and the American imperialists ... You must work hard to produce much ... We are building the only true Communism ... Our Communism will be better than in Russia or China where there are still classes ... You are now free ... You are happy ... Give up all your material possessions, for now they belong to Angka ...'

From John Barron and Anthony Paul, *Peace with Horror*, Hodder and Stoughton, 1977.

---

1 According to source G, what were the aims of Angka Loeu in creating New Villages?
2 Bearing in mind that this report is based on accounts by refugees from New Villages, how reliable do you think it is as evidence of conditions in Communist-run Cambodia?

Using the sources in this chapter as evidence, make a list of issues that led to conflict in Indo-China between 1945 and 1975.

15　The Great Society? The USA since 1945

At the end of the Second World War in 1945, the United States of America returned to what it had been doing in the 'roaring twenties'; making itself into the world's leading industrial nation, and its people into the world's richest. While the peoples of Europe, the USSR, China and Japan were sorting out the rubble of their shattered cities, the Americans went straight into an economic boom in which the pent-up demand for consumer goods created by war-time shortages and high war-time wages led to rapid industrial growth.

A booming economy was not the only echo of the roaring twenties to be heard in the post-war years, however. The world's richest people continued after 1945 to be divided by conflicts over their political and religious beliefs, over their race relations and civil rights, and over the extent to which the federal government should concern itself with the lives of individual Americans or with the affairs of the fifty states. The sources in this chapter have been chosen to illustrate each of those conflicts.

The first conflict was a political one, and it revolved around the Republican Senator from Wisconsin, Joseph McCarthy. From 1950 to 1954 McCarthy ran a campaign against alleged Communists in the government, claiming that they had helped Communists to take power in China in 1949, and that they were betraying their country's secrets to the Soviet Union. 'McCarthyism' ruined the reputations of many leading Democratic politicians and intellectuals and helped to bring about the defeat of the Democrats in the 1952 Presidential election. Its success depended to a great extent on the manner in which McCarthy accused his victims of involvement with Communist organisations. His methods can be seen in this extract from a speech he made to the Republican Party Convention in October 1952, attacking Adlai Stevenson, the Democratic candidate in the Presidential elections due to be held the following month:

A We are at war tonight – a war which started decades ago, a war which we did not start, a war which we cannot stop except by either victory or death. The Korean War is only one phase of this war between international atheistic communism and our free civilisation.

And we've been losing, we've been losing that war since the shooting part of World War Two ended, losing it at an incredibly fantastic rate of 100,000,000 people a year.

And for the past two and a half years I've been trying to expose and force out of high positions in Government those who are in charge of our deliberate planned retreat from victory....

And tonight, tonight I shall give you the history of the Democratic candidate for the Presidency who endorsed and could continue the suicidal Kremlin-directed policies of the nation....

The time is short, so let me get about the task of looking at his record. The Democratic candidate has said, and I quote him verbatim. He said 'As evidence of my direction I have established my headquarters here in Springfield with people of my own choosing.' In other words he says, judge me, judge me by the advisers I have selected. Good, let's do that. Let's examine a few of those advisers first.

First is Wilson Wyatt, his personal manager. Now Wilson Wyatt is a former head of the left-winger A.D.A., the Americans for Democratic Action. . . .

Next, and perhaps the key figure in the Stevenson camp, is his speech writer, Arthur Schlesinger Jr, former vice-Chairman of the A.D.A. Now, Schlesinger has been a writer, incidentally, for the New York Post whose editor and his wife admit, admit that they were members of the Young Communist League. . . .

The next – one of the men selected by Stevenson as one of his ghost writers – is a man Jim, James Wechsler. Wechsler and his wife both admit – both admit having been members of the Young Communist League. . . .

Another of the men in the Democratic candidate's camp is Archibald Macleish. . . .

Well, how does this man Macleish – he's got that – the longest record of affiliation with Communist fronts of any man I have ever named in Washington. And Adlai says, Judge me by the friends I select. To that I say 'Amen, Adlai, Amen.'

From Barton J. Bernstein and Allen J. Matusow (eds.), *The Truman Administration: A Documentary History*, Harper and Row, 1966.

1 What, according to the first three paragraphs of his speech, were McCarthy's aims?
2 What accusations does McCarthy make against Wilson Wyatt, Arthur Schlesinger Jr, James Wechsler and Archibald Macleish?
3 How does McCarthy use those accusations to discredit Adlai Stevenson?
4 How convincing do you find the accusations? Explain your answer.

Although McCarthy's accusations were usually groundless, he attracted a huge following and created a 'red scare' that kept the United States in a state of anti-Communist hysteria for several years. One of his opponents, the journalist Richard Rovere, explained his popularity in a biography published in 1959:

B At a typical McCarthy rally there would be, seated in the front rows, thanks to early arrival, numbers of moon-struck souls wearing badges or carrying placards identifying them as Minute Women of the U.S.A., Sons of I Shall Return, members of the Alert Council for America, and Nationalist Action League, We the Mothers Mobilise, the Republoform, and so on. They knew all the words of 'Nobody loves Joe but the Pee-pul,' and if this anthem was sung, their voices, generally on the shrill or reedy side, would be heard above the rest. But this was really the least part of it. McCarthy went far beyond the world of the daft and the frenzied. . . . Into it came large numbers of Republicans who had coolly decided that there was no longer any respectable way of unhorsing the Democrats and that only McCarthy's wild and conscienceless policies could do the job.

From Richard Rovere, *Senator Joe McCarthy*, Methuen, 1960.

1 How does Richard Rovere suggest that many of McCarthy's supporters belonged to the 'lunatic fringe' of American politics?

2 According to Richard Rovere, what was the main reason for McCarthy's popularity among Republicans?

3 What criticisms can be made of source B as a piece of historical explanation?

'McCarthyism' died out in the mid-1950s after McCarthy discredited himself by attacking the United States armed forces as well as President Eisenhower. But no sooner had this conflict disappeared from the American scene than another took its place. This was a conflict between black and white people, and between southern state governments and the federal government, over the issue of civil rights.

The issue of civil rights came to the forefront of American politics in 1954, when the Supreme Court of the USA ruled that states should allow black children to attend the same schools as white children so that they could have equal opportunities and facilities. Until then, black children in the southern states had been restricted to segregated schools such as the one shown in this photograph taken in 1949:

C

Source: *Life Magazine.*

15. The Great Society? The USA since 1945

115

1 Roughly how many children are there in this school? What does their age range appear to be?
2 What educational disadvantages were these children likely to suffer?
3 For what purposes could a civil rights campaigner have used this photograph?
4 What might a white opponent of civil rights campaigners have said in response to seeing this picture?

The Supreme Court's decision angered many white Americans in the southern states, where there was a powerful tradition of racial prejudice against black people. The full ugliness of their prejudice was seen in September 1957 when nine black school students attempted to start the new school year at the previously all-white Central High School in Little Rock, Arkansas. This account was written by a white journalist, Benjamin Fine, and published in the *New York Times* on 24 September 1957:

D At eight o'clock it was evident that the violence that Governor Faubus had predicted would take place. By this time some five hundred persons had gathered. They appeared in a fighting mood.

'The niggers* won't get in,' members of the crowd said time and time again.

* black people

At eight forty-five the school buzzer could be dimly heard. School was in session.

'Where are the niggers?' one person asked another. 'Let them try to get in. . . .'

'We'll lynch* them all,' several yelled.

* hang

'Sure, and all you Yankee newspapermen with them,' a gravel-voiced man shouted. This was met with a howl of approval. . . .

Suddenly a yell went up. 'There they are, they're coming!'

A man yelled: 'Look, they're going into our school.'

Six girls and three boys crossed over into the school yard. They had arrived in two automobiles and had driven to the side of the school. . . .

Slowly, almost as though they were entering a normal classroom on a normal school day, the students walked toward the side door of the school. The boys, in open shirts, and the girls, in bobbysocks, joked and chatted among themselves. They carried armfuls of textbooks.

The crowd now let out a roar of rage. 'They've gone in,' a man shouted.

'Oh God,' said a woman, 'the niggers are in school.'

A group of six girls, dressed in skirts and sweaters, hair in ponytails, started to shriek and wail.

'The niggers are in our school,' they howled hysterically.

One of them jumped up and down on the sidewalk, waving her arms toward her classmates in the school who were looking out of the windows, and screamed over and over again, 'Come on out, come on out.'

Tears flowed down her face, her body shook in uncontrollable spasms. Three of her classmates grew hysterical and threw their arms around each other. They began dancing up and down.

'The niggers are in,' they shrieked, 'come on out of the school. Don't stay there with the niggers. Come on out, come on.' . . .

By twelve o'clock the mob had reached its greatest strength, and by now completely ignored the local police. The crowd remained behind the barricade, but it did not maintain order there. Several newsmen were kicked and beaten. A negro reporter was kicked and manhandled.

Threats, jeers and insults became more ominous.

'Let's rush the police,' a ringleader shouted. 'They can't stop us.'

At noon the police received this message on their short-wave radios: 'This is the Mayor. Tell Principal Jeff Meadows* that the Negroes have been withdrawn. Tell Mr. Matthews to announce that to the student body. I've talked with Virgil Blossom† and the Negroes have been withdrawn.' . . .

*Head of Central High School
†Superintendent of Schools
From Anthony Lewis, The Second American Revolution: A First-Hand Account of the Struggle for Civil Rights, Faber and Faber, 1966.

---

1 What impressions does the reporter create of (a) the demonstrators, and (b) the nine black students? Quote from his report to illustrate your answer.
2 Suggest why the demonstrators kicked and beat several of the newsmen.
3 Do you think that this report is an impartial account of events, or does the reporter reveal his sympathies in any way? Explain your answer.
4 Assuming that the report is a reasonably accurate picture of events, why do you think that the demonstrators behaved in the ugly ways described?

By the early 1960s the campaign for civil rights had developed into a major protest movement with a massive following. Organisations such as the NAACP (National Association for the Advancement of Coloured People) and CORE (Congress on Racial Equality) mounted impressive non-violent campaigns aimed at desegregating public transport, education and public places in the southern states. But any progress they made was slow and hard-won. By the time a major Civil Rights Act was passed in 1964, many black people had joined more extreme organisations, such as the Black Panthers, which were prepared to go beyond non-violent campaigning in pursuit of their rights. In many cases this led to conflict with the police, especially in the cities where a series of 'race riots' took place in the mid-1960s. The first of the riots took place in Harlem, New York, only two weeks after the 1964 Civil Rights Act had become law. How the riot started is described here by Paul Montgomery, a reporter for the New York Times:

E A few minutes before seven o'clock Saturday night, a young woman from the Congress of Racial Equality [CORE] set up a rickety blue café chair and a child's American flag on the southwest corner of 125th Street and Seventh Avenue. A desultory crowd of a hundred gathered in the steaming early evening and the rally began. . . .

The rally was sponsored by three militant CORE chapters – Downtown, East River and South Jamaica. Its purpose had originally been to protest events in Mississippi, but the theme shifted after Thursday morning, when Lieutenant Thomas Gilligan shot and killed 15-year-old James Powell in an apartment house doorway on East 76th Street. . . .

A dozen patrolmen lounged and watched from nearby stations as Judith Howell, a 17-year-old member of Bronx CORE spoke to the crowd from the blue chair. 'James Powell was shot because he was black,' the girl said. The crowd murmured assent and applauded. 'We got a civil rights bill,' she went on, 'and along with the bill we got Barry Goldwater* and a dead boy.'

an outspoken Republican candidate in the Presidential election of 1964

The shifting crowd had grown to about two hundred. Several of them heckled the CORE speakers who followed. 'White people dictate your policy,' one man yelled. Chris Sprowal, chairman of Downtown CORE, said 'It is time to let "the man"* know that if he does something to us we are going to do something back. If you say, "You kick me once, I'm going to kick you twice", we might get some respect.' Charles Saunders of South Jamaica CORE followed with the charge that 'forty-five per cent of the cops in New York are neurotic murderers.' The crowd grew more excited, but not unruly. Then CORE turned over the blue chair to the speakers in the crowd.

white people

At about eight p.m. the Reverend Nelson C. Dukes of the Fountain Springs Baptist Church, 15 West 126th Street, mounted the makeshift podium and gave a twenty-minute speech. Declaring it was time to stop talking and to act, he shouted that the people on the rally should march to the police station and present their demands. The crowd became more animated. There were shouts of 'Let's go' and 'Let's do it now.' A scar-faced man wearing a white sports shirt followed the preacher, saying 'We have got to act now.' . . .

A few bottles and garbage-can covers sailed towards the police. The policemen donned helmets and faced the crowd. The crowd began taunting the policemen as some patrolmen rushed to the rooftops to stop the bottle throwing.

New York Police Commissioner

'Murphy* must be removed', the crowd shouted. 'Killers, murderers, Murphy's rats.'

From Anthony Lewis, *The Second American Revolution: A First-Hand Account of the Struggle for Civil Rights*, Faber and Faber, 1966.

---

1 Why were the people attending the rally angry?

2 Why did the rally become violent?

3 What evidence is there in source E that some black people were dissatisfied with the policies of established protest groups like CORE?

Lyndon Baines Johnson, US President from 1963 to 1968, did much to try to improve the conditions of disadvantaged Americans. The Civil Rights Act of 1964, the Education Act of 1965, the establishment of

'Medicare' and of the Office of Economic Opportunity were key elements in his plan to create a 'Great Society'. All too often, however, Johnson was prevented from carrying through his reforms by conservative Democrats in his own party as well as by his Republican opponents in Congress. Johnson recounted one such occasion in his memoirs:

F July 20, 1967, was another day when conservatives mounted an attack, this time a day of shame and defeat. On that day a simple, uncomplicated bill came before the House of Representatives which proposed to provide federal grants to local neighbourhoods for developing and carrying out rat control and extermination methods. . . .

Every year thousands of people, especially those living in the slums of our cities, are bitten by rats in their homes and tenements. The overwhelming majority of victims are babies lying in their cribs. Some of them die of their wounds. Many are disfigured for life. . . .

But the greatest damage cannot be measured in objective terms. You cannot measure the demoralising effect that the plague of rats has on human beings – a mother awakened by a cry in the middle of the night to find her child bleeding with rat bites on his nose, lips or ears . . . – the disgust, fear and hatred intrinsic to rodent-infested warrens of substandard living.

It was mid-afternoon when House Resolution 749 reached the floor. The resolution was a rule to consider the Rat Extermination and Control Act of 1967. Everything seemed in order for quick and easy passage of the bill. But something happened in the House that afternoon, something shameful and sad. A handful of Republicans joined together not merely to defeat the bill but to make low comedy of the entire program. Congressman Joel Broyhill, a Republican from Virginia, helped set the tone: 'Mr Speaker, I think the "rat smart thing" for us to do is to vote down this rat bill "rat now"'.

The floodgates opened. The House, as it is prone to do on occasion, had a field day – laughing about high commissioners of rats, hordes of rat bureaucrats . . . jesting about the new civil 'rats' bill, 'throwing money down a rathole', and discriminating between city and country rats. At the end of this burlesque the rat bill was defeated by a vote of 207 to 176. The old Republican-conservative-Democratic coalition had won again.

From Lyndon Baines Johnson, *The Vantage Point: Perspectives of the Presidency 1963–69*, Weidenfeld and Nicolson, 1972.

---

1 What light does source F throw on living conditions in American cities in the 1960s?
2 How reliable do you consider source F as evidence of living conditions in American cities in the 1960s?
3 How might one of the 207 Congressmen who voted against the rat bill have explained his reasons for opposing it?
4 What light does source F throw on the difficulties that an American President can face when trying to introduce new laws?

The divisions in American society illustrated by sources A to F have not entirely disappeared. Some are as deep as ever, as source G shows. It is part of a publicity 'mailshot' put out by a political and religious organisation called 'The Moral Majority' in 1985:

G Is Our Grand Old Flag Going Down The Drain?
Dear Friend,

I have bad news for you:

The answer to the question above is 'YES!'
Our grand old flag is going down the drain. Don't kid yourself. You may wake up some morning and discover that Old Glory is no longer waving freely.

Just look at what's happening here in America:
- Known practising homosexual teachers have invaded the classrooms, and the pulpits of our churches.
- Smut pedlars sell their pornographic books – under the protection of the courts!
- And X-rated movies are allowed in almost every community because there is no legal definition of obscenity.
- Meanwhile, right in our own homes the television screen is full of R-rated movies and sex and violence.
- Believe it or not, we are the first civilised nation in history to legalise abortion – in the late months of pregnancy! Murder!

How long can all this go on?

I repeat: Our grand old flag is going down the drain. . . .
And unless we rebuild our military strength and keep a careful watch over the strength of our military position . . .
. . . one day the Russians may be able to pick up the telephone and call Washington, D.C., and dictate the terms of our surrender. And when that happens – Old Glory is down the drain, forever.
Is God finished with America? I don't believe He is . . . But time is short: and that is why I am writing this letter to you.
I believe that the overwhelming majority of Americans are sick and tired of the way the amoral liberals are trying to corrupt our nation from its commitment to freedom, democracy, traditional morality, and the free enterprise system . . .

From The Moral Majority Inc.,
Washington, DC., 1985.

---

1 What similarities are there between the opinions expressed in this letter and the opinions expressed in source A? In what ways is source A dissimilar?
2 What kind of person do you think this letter was trying to attract?

Using sources A to G in this chapter, explain why American society since 1945 has been divided by:
1 racial conflicts, 2 political conflicts, 3 conflicts over moral issues.

16   The USSR without Stalin: the Soviet Union since 1953

Joseph Stalin, dictator of the Soviet Union for twenty-five years, died after a stroke in March 1953. Soviet people reacted to his death in different ways. Some breathed deep sighs of relief; others wept openly in grief; many were simply stunned by the news. But few people failed to react at all.

In Moscow, immense crowds of mourners made their way to Red Square, hoping to view his body lying in state. The Soviet poet Yevgeni Yevtushenko was among the crowds, and he later wrote about what happened that day:

A A sort of paralysis came over the country. People who had been trained to believe that Stalin was taking care of everyone, were lost and bewildered without him. The whole of Russia wept. So did I.

I'll never forget going to see Stalin's coffin. The breath of thousands of people pressed against one another rose up in a thick white cloud. The crowd turned into a monstrous whirlpool.

I realised that I was being carried (by the crowd) straight towards a traffic light. Suddenly I saw that a young girl was being pushed against the post. Her face was distorted by a despairing scream. A movement of the crowd drove me against the girl; I did not hear but felt with my body the cracking of her brittle bones as they were broken on the traffic light.

I closed my eyes in horror and I was swept past. When I looked again, the girl was no longer to be seen. The crowd must have sucked her under.

At that moment I felt I was treading on something soft. It was a human body. I picked my feet up and was borne along by the crowd. I was saved by my height. Short people were smothered alive. We were caught between the walls of houses on one side and a row of army trucks of the other.

'Get the trucks out of the way!' people howled.

'I can't. I've got no instructions,' a very young, bewildered police officer shouted back from one of the trucks. And people were being hurled against the trucks by the crowd, and their heads smashed. The sides of the trucks were running with blood.

All at once I felt a savage hatred for everything that had given birth to that 'No instructions' shouted when people were dying of someone's stupidity. For the first time in my life I thought with hatred of the man we were burying. He could not be innocent of the disaster.

From Yevgeni Yevtushenko, *A Precocious Autobiography*, Collins and Harvill Press, 1963.

---

1 What does this account tell us about the feelings of Soviet people for Stalin?
2 What do you think Yevtushenko meant by 'everything that had given birth to that "No instructions"'?
3 Why did Yevtushenko blame Stalin for the disaster?
4 How reliable a witness of these events do you consider Yevtushenko? Explain your answer.

After Stalin's death the leading members of the Politburo, the policy-making body of the Communist Party, governed the Soviet Union in a collective leadership. One of them, First Party Secretary Nikita Khrushchev, later recalled the situation they faced in their first months of power:

B Stalin was dead and buried, but ... Stalinist policies were still in force.... For three years we were unable to break with the past, unable to muster the courage and the determination to lift the curtain and see what had been hidden from us about the arrests, the trials, the arbitrary rule, the executions, and everything else that had happened during Stalin's reign. It was as though we were enchained by our own activities under Stalin's leadership, and couldn't free ourselves from his control even after he was dead ... We couldn't imagine that all those executions during the purges were, from a legal standpoint, crimes themselves. But it was true! Criminal acts had been committed by Stalin, acts which would be punishable in any state in the world except in fascist states like Hitler's and Mussolini's.

From N. S. Khrushchev, *Khrushchev Remembers* (translated and edited by Strobe Talbott), André Deutsch, 1971.

---

1 What impression does Khrushchev give of the Soviet Union under Stalin in source B?
2 How does the impression created by Khrushchev agree with that created by Yevtushenko in source A?

By 1956 Khrushchev had emerged as the most important member of the collective leadership. His position, however, was not yet unshakeable. In order to become the undisputed single leader of the Soviet Union, he had not only to defeat senior rivals such as Malenkov and Molotov, but also to free the country from the grip of Stalin's dead hand. Khrushchev began this task of 'Destalinisation' by attacking Stalin's record and reputation in a four-hour speech at the Twentieth Congress of the Communist Party in 1956. Khrushchev was so outspoken in his criticisms of Stalin that, it is said, thirty of the 1600 delegates listening to him fainted or had seizures. The following extracts from the speech help to explain why:

C (i) Lenin's traits – patient work with people; stubborn and painstaking education of them; the ability to induce people to follow him without using compulsion ... were entirely foreign to Stalin. He [Stalin] discarded the Leninist method of convincing and educating for that of administrative violence, mass repressions and terror. He acted on an increasingly larger scale ... often violating all existing norms of morality and of Soviet laws.... Mass arrests and deportations of many thousands of people, execution without trial and without normal investigation created conditions of insecurity, fear and even desperation.

(ii) Stalin was a very distrustful man, sickly suspicious; we knew this from our work with him. He could look at a man and say: 'Why are your eyes so shifty today,' or 'Why are you turning so much today and avoiding to look me directly in the eyes?' The sickly suspicion created in him a general distrust even toward eminent Party workers whom he had known for years. Everywhere and in everything he saw 'enemies,' 'two-facers,' and 'spies'. . . .

(iii) The power accumulated in the hands of one person, Stalin, led to serious consequences during the Great Patriotic War. . . . The necessary steps were not taken to prepare the country properly for defence and to prevent it being caught unawares. Did we have time and the capabilities for such preparations? Yes, we had the time and capabilities. Our industry was already so developed that it was capable of supplying the Soviet army with everything it needed. . . . Had our industry been mobilised properly and in time to supply the army with the necessary *matériel*, our wartime losses would have been decidedly smaller. Such mobilisation had not been, however, started in time. . . .

(iv) And what were the results of this carefree attitude, this disregard of clear facts? The result was that already in the first hours and days the enemy had destroyed in our border regions a large part of our air force, artillery and other military equipment. . . . Even after the war began, the nervousness and hysteria which Stalin demonstrated, interfering with actual military operations, caused our army serious damage. Stalin was very far from understanding the real situation which was developing at the front. This was natural because during the whole Patriotic War he never visited any section of the front or any liberated city except for one short ride on the Mozhaisk Highway during a stabilised situation at the front. . . .

(v) We must state that after the war . . . Stalin became ever more capricious, irritable and brutal; in particular his suspicion grew. His persecution mania reached unbelievable dimensions. Many workers were becoming enemies before his very eyes. After the war Stalin separated himself from the collective even more. Everything was decided by him alone without any consideration for anyone or anything. . . .

(vi) Comrades: We must abolish the cult of the individual decisively, once and for all. . . .

From N. S. Khrushchev, *Khrushchev Remembers* (translated and edited by Strobe Talbott), André Deutsch, 1971.

---

1 What criticisms of Stalin did Khrushchev make in this speech?

2 Describe Stalin's character as it emerges from source C. Quote from the source to illustrate the characteristics you mention.

3 Why do you think many of the delegates listening to Khrushchev's speech were shocked by what they heard?

Khrushchev's speech to the Twentieth Party Congress was a turning point in the post-war development of the Soviet Union. Mass terror was dropped as a method of government, and although the secret police, the labour camps, the censorship, and all the other methods of terror remained in existence, they were used less rigorously. One result of this was a slight 'thaw' in the Soviet Union's cultural life; writers and poets, painters and musicians, artists of all kinds were able to express themselves more freely than at any time in the past twenty-five years. An example of the new freedom allowed to artists was the publication in 1962 of Alexander Solzhenitsyn's novel about Stalinist prison camps, *One Day in the Life of Ivan Denisovitch*. Source D is a passage from the novel, describing the reasons for Ivan Denisov-itch's imprisonment in a Siberian labour camp.

D According to his dossier, Ivan Denisovitch Shukhov had been sentenced for high treason. He had testified to it himself. Yes, he'd surrendered to the Germans with the intention of betraying his country and he'd returned from captivity to carry out a mission for German intelligence. What sort of mission neither Shukhov nor the interrogator could say. So it had been left at that – a mission.

Shukhov reckoned simply. If he didn't sign he'd be shot. If he signed he'd still get a chance to live. So he signed.

But what really happened was this. In February 1942 their whole army was surrounded on the north-west front. No food was para-chuted to them. There were no planes. Things got so bad that they were scraping the hooves of dead horses – the horn could be soaked in water and eaten. They'd no ammunition left. So the Germans rounded them up in the forest, a few at a time. Shukhov was in one of these groups, and remained in German captivity for a day or two. Then five of them managed to escape. They stole through the forest and marshes again, and, by a miracle, reached their own lines. A tommy-gunner shot two of them on the spot, a third died of his wounds, but two got through. Had they been wiser they'd have said they'd been wandering about the forest, and then nothing would have happened. But they told the truth: they said they were escaped p.o.w.s. P.o.w.s, you fuckers! If five of them had got through, their statements could have been found to tally and they might have been believed. But with two it was hopeless. You've put your bloody heads together and cooked up that escape story, they were told.

From Alexander Solzhenitsyn, *One Day in the Life of Ivan Denisovitch*, Gollancz, 1963.

---

1 Why would the novel from which source D is taken not have been published while Stalin was alive?

2 How far does this extract support Khrushchev's accusations against Stalin in source C?

3 Solzhenitsyn based this novel on his own experience of imprisonment in a Stalinist labour camp; do you therefore consider it a reliable source of evidence about Stalinist labour camps, even though it is fiction? Explain your answer.

During the two years after his 1956 speech, Khrushchev completed the process of 'Destalinisation' by driving what he called an 'anti-Party Group' of old Stalin supporters out of the Politburo, and then by getting rid of Bulganin, the Prime Minister. By 1958 Khrushchev had supreme power. In the internal affairs of the Soviet Union, Khrushchev used this power primarily to change the way in which the Soviet economy was run. Source E, taken from the Programme of the Communist Party of the Soviet Union (CPSU) drawn up in 1961, shows some of the basic aims of Soviet economic policy under Khrushchev:

E The heroic labour of the Soviet people has produced a powerful and versatile economy. There is now every possibility to improve rapidly the living standards of the entire population – the workers, peasants and intellectuals. The CPSU puts forward the historically important task of achieving in the Soviet Union a living standard higher than that of any of the capitalist countries.

The task will be effected by (a) raising individual payment according to the quantity and quality of work done, coupled with reduction of retail prices and abolition of taxes paid by the population: (b) increase of the public consumption fund intended for ... free of charge education, medical treatment, pensions, maintenance of children at children's institutions, transition to cost-free use of public amenities, etc. ...

Soviet people will be more prosperous than working people in the developed capitalist countries even if average incomes are equal, because in the Soviet Union the national income is distributed in the interests of all members of society and there are no parasitical classes as in the bourgeois countries who appropriate and squander immense wealth plundered from millions of working people.

From *The Programme of the Communist Party of the Soviet Union*, October 1961.

---

1 What, according to source E, were the main economic aims of the Soviet Union in 1961?
2 In what ways are these aims similar to the economic aims of non-Communist countries? In what ways are they different?

To encourage the Soviet people to achieve such aims, the Communist Party used all sorts of propaganda, particularly large posters. Source F is an example of this, a poster seen in 'Our Motherland', a collective farm in the southern USSR visited in 1972 by a British journalist:

F 'FURTHER INTENSIFY SOCIALIST COMPETITION FOR FULFILMENT OF THE FIVE-YEAR PLAN BEFORE SCHEDULE! WHEN HARVESTING WHEAT, REMEMBER: A LOST DAY CANNOT BE MADE UP IN A YEAR! THE DUTY OF EVERY AGRICULTURAL WORKER, DEPUTY TO THE SOVIET, AND HOUSEWIFE, PIONEER* AND SCHOOL CHILD: BAR THE WAY TO WEEDS ON ALL FIELDS! WE ARE APPROACHING THE VICTORY OF COMMUNIST LABOUR! GLORY TO LABOUR! LIQUIDATION OF THE

* *The Young Pioneers: a Communist Party youth organisation*

DIFFERENCES IN SOCIAL, ECONOMIC, CULTURAL AND LIVING STAN-
DARDS BETWEEN CITY AND COUNTRY IS ONE OF THE GREATEST
ACHIEVEMENTS IN THE BUILDING OF COMMUNISM.'

From George Feifer, *Russia Close-Up*,
Jonathan Cape, 1973.

---

1 What does source F reveal about the economic problems still being experienced by the USSR in 1972?
2 What else does source F tell you about the USSR in 1972?

How far has the Soviet economy achieved the aims set by the Communist Party in 1961? We can look for answers to that question in the mountains of statistics produced not only by the Soviet government but also by foreign economic observers. Sources G and H are two such sets of statistics. Study them carefully before answering the questions on the next page:

G Retail prices of goods and services shown in minutes of work-time* in 1979

Item	Washington	Moscow	Munich	Paris	London
1 kilo of white bread	8	18	5	14	12
1 kilo of rye bread	20	12	7	34	12
1 kilo of chicken	14	223	19	35	34
1 kilo of beef mince	43	128	48	73	57
1 kilo of pork sausages	31	145	40	53	43
100 g milk chocolate	7	77	6	7	13
1 kilo of butter	47	237	45	53	57
1 litre of fresh milk	7	18	5	6	9
10 large eggs	10	99	11	23	20
1 kilo of carrots	7	10	6	9	11
1 kilo of potatoes	2	7	2	4	4
1 kilo of apples	11	40	8	8	15
1 kilo of oranges	6	92	8	8	16
100 g of instant coffee	16	395	24	32	32
100 tea bags	26	197	24	44	29
1 litre of beer	8	20	7	10	22
0.5 litre of vodka	52	380	54	105	161
20 cigarettes	9	23	16	7	22
Car (months of work-time)	4	35	7	8	9
3 kilometre bus ride	5	3	5	4	9
Rent (hours of work-time)	53	12	25	44	23
1 month's electricity	195	138	186	166	392
1 month's telephone hire	169	55	162	207	123
1 month's water rates	—	8	30	44	112

From Leonard Shapiro and Joseph Godson (eds.), *The Soviet Worker, Illusions and Realities*, Macmillan, 1981.

* the length of time a person must work in order to earn the cost of the item

H Industrial output in the Soviet Union, 1940–1979

Product	1940	1965	1979
Electricity (million MWh)	49	507	1239
Oil (million tonnes)	31	243	586
Natural gas (cubic kilometres)	3	128	407
Coal (million tonnes)	166	578	719
Steel (million tonnes)	18	91	149
Mineral fertiliser (million tonnes)	3	31	95
Synthetic fibres (thousand tonnes)	11	407	1100
Metal cutting machine tools (thousands)	58	186	231
Lorries (thousands)	136	380	780
Motor cars (thousands)	6	201	1314
Tractors (thousands)	32	355	557
Paper (million tonnes)	1	3	5
Cement (million tonnes)	6	72	123
Cotton (million square metres)	2715	5499	6974
Wool (million square metres)	155	466	774
Leather footwear (million pairs)	211	486	739

From Archie Brown, John Fennell *et al.* (eds.) *The Cambridge Encyclopaedia of Russia and the Soviet Union,* Cambridge University Press, 1982.

---

1 In general, do the figures in source H support the view expressed in source E that the Soviet Union had a 'powerful and versatile economy' by the 1960s?

2 How does the table in source G suggest that the Soviet Union had achieved 'a living standard higher than that of any of the capitalist countries'?

3 How does source G suggest that the Soviet Union had not achieved this aim?

Historians cannot rely on statistics alone when they investigate questions of economic history. People's experiences may suggest a very different picture from that painted by statistics. Source I is one such picture. It was written in 1980 by Fyodor Turovsky, a Russian lawyer who emigrated from the Soviet Union in 1976 to live in Canada:

I My first taste of working class life in the West came in the Montreal flat of Boris Sklyarsky, a sewing machine mechanic who had emigrated from Leningrad. He invited me to visit him because I had only just arrived from Moscow, to talk about the old days in Russia and explain a few things about this world so new and unfamiliar for a Soviet émigré.

'Well, how are you finding things in your new country?' I asked, expecting a torrent of enthusiastic praise in reply.

'Oh, nothing special', he replied flatly, and added: 'In any case, we're no better off here than we were in the Soviet Union.'

'But you have to admit that you earn a lot more here', I persisted.

'Not at all; I earn less here in Canada.' My astonishment was so obvious that Boris did not wait for more questions, but hastened to make himself clear. 'Forgive me, but your question was about earnings, not about actual wages, and the two are very different things you know. Here in Montreal I work in a clothes factory. I get 300 dollars a week. Then I mend people's machines at home, that gives me another 100 dollars a week. My wife works in a library and gets 200 dollars a week. Together, that makes between 2400 and 2500 dollars a month.'

'But there you are, then! As a mechanic, you wouldn't have earned more than 150 roubles a month in the Soviet Union!'

'Even less, actually 120–130 roubles, but I had another bread-winner: my Volga* which brought in 100 roubles and more in one evening, working on the side. That meant not less than 3000 a month! I had my permanent clientele – black marketeers who had to move their merchandise. They would be afraid to call a taxi in case the driver turned out to be a KGB man, and that would mean playing straight into the authorities' hands. They'd pay two or three hundred for just one trip, depending on what the load was. Textiles and footwear paid more, fruit less, because the risks involved were less. I made four or five roubles a month, on average.'

a make of Russian car

'What do you mean, four or five roubles?'

'Four or five thousand of course . . .'

'I suppose petrol was expensive?' I enquired.

'Petrol was dirt cheap back at home. No energy crisis over there, you know! Any lorry driver will be only too happy to siphon a hundred litres into your tank for the price of a bottle of vodka. . . .'

'But when all's said and done, are you happy to be rid of all that?'

'Well . . .' said Boris, considering the matter. 'Sure I'm happy that I can earn enough at my job to live well, very well. But of course there are other problems. We don't speak the language properly, and probably never will. We've left behind our families and friends, here we'll have to find new ones, and that's not so simple. We had lots of little pleasures over there which we'll never see the like of again. If you managed through some acquaintance to get hold of some beer, or a bottle of "Stolichnaya"* that was a great occasion. If it was meat or fish, then you were over the moon. Everyone here talks English or French so fast there's no hope of understanding them. That's when you start feeling homesick, and homesickness is a terrible disease, not something that can be cured by bananas and tomatoes. Of course it's sad for a Russian to leave Russia; but it's not Russia he's leaving, not Russia as it could have been and as it should have been – it's a prison he's leaving, and even if they fed him well in prison, it was still a prison. I left behind my flat, my Volga, my safe job and salary, and emigrated, because that's no way to live.'

a brand of vodka

From Leonard Shapiro and Joseph Godson (eds.), *The Soviet Worker, Illusions and Realities*, Macmillan, 1981.

1 How does source I suggest that living standards in the Soviet Union were equal to, or higher than those in Canada?

2 (a) What is a 'black marketeer'?

  (b) According to source I, what goods were bought and sold on the black market?

  (c) Judging by source G, can you suggest why this was so?

3 What problems of daily life in the Soviet Union are revealed by source I?

4 Why might the writer of source I be accused of bias? Does this affect the value of source I as historical evidence? Explain your answer.

Compare sources A to D with sources F to I, then answer these questions:

1 What major changes have taken place in Soviet life since the death of Stalin?

2 In what respects does life seem not to have changed?

17 'Liberation': China after 1949

When the Chinese talk about the Communist seizure of power in 1949, they call it 'Liberation'. By this they mean that Mao Zedong's new Communist government liberated China from poverty, inequality, ignorance and many other injustices of traditional Chinese society.

Some of the ways in which Liberation changed the lives of city people can be seen in this account by Chow Qingli, the wife of a Shanghai businessman:

A Within three years of the Liberation, life in cities like Shanghai was completely different. The teachers, missionaries, bankers and businessmen from Europe and America were now only a memory. . . . The big foreign cars had gone. Instead vast numbers of bicycles had appeared. All of China's people, from old men to children, had begun a big clean-up – against rats, flies and mosquitoes. Each family was asked to produce a weekly number of rat tails, at least one rat tail per member of the family. Those who beat the required number were allowed to have a small red flag on their front door. Soon there were red flags all over the place.

Another change was that beggars disappeared almost overnight. Before 1949 they had been a normal sight at every street corner.

One of the most dramatic changes that took place, and one that made me weep bitterly, was Mao's Marriage Reform Law. This came only five months after my own (forced) marriage ... The old marriage system which allowed forced or arranged marriages and which made women the servants of their men is now abolished. All marriages are to be based on the free consent of men and women. . . .

Mao also banned other horrible practices such as the drowning of newborn female babies, polygamy and the selling of women as servants or prostitutes. Mass meetings and campaigns were held throughout the city to explain the laws. . . .

In general those who had most reason to fear the PLA* – the warlords, bankers and corrupt officials – had already fled to Taiwan. Those who stayed behind found at first that they could carry on with business as usual. The government badly wanted to persuade the capitalists to start to rebuild . . . . I myself was one of the richest women in Shanghai. The government needed the money and expert knowledge of businessmen.

* People's Liberation Army

Quoted in C.K. Macdonald, *Modern China*, Basil Blackwell, 1985.

---

1 According to Chow Qingli, who benefited from Liberation in 1949? Who did not benefit?

2 Why do you think the Marriage Reform Law made her weep?

3 In what ways does Chow Qingli suggest that the Communist government had widespread public support in the years immediately after Liberation?

Liberation had equally dramatic effects on the lives of China's peasants, the majority of the population. In source B an old man named Hsi-Kun talks about his life in Upper Felicity, a northern Chinese village, before and after Liberation. His memories were recorded by Jack Chen, an overseas Chinese journalist from Trinidad, who spent 1970 living in Upper Felicity.

B There were over sixty families in this hamlet before Liberation, and whether they were poor or lower-middle peasants, they were all poor. Only a few families could keep their heads above water, and only the landlord and a couple of other rich peasants could sleep nights in peace. Apart from these few the whole hamlet owned only eight oxen. When flood, drought or famine came it would send most of us fleeing with everything we could carry. Many never got back. Those were bad days. Bitter! Homes were ruined. Families broken up. Once in such a time of calamity, an old woman died and not eight men could be found to carry her coffin to the grave.

Taxes were heavy. If you didn't pay your tax, those reactionaries would take away your windows, one by one, and sell the timber; then your door, and even the roof beams so that the roof fell down. If you borrowed grain to pay the tax, it was like hanging stones around the neck of a drowning man to save him. You had to pay back five *tou* for every one you borrowed.

If you hadn't paid the tax and the authorities heard you had a little food laid by, they came and seized it. We were never able to pay the tax in full or keep up with the interest payments on our debts, and we were always being persecuted for the one thing or the other. Once my father tried to run away from it all, but they caught him before he had got very far. They brought him back, tied him up, and strung him up all night from a beam. . . .

Sometimes the reactionary government (he meant the Guomindang government or whatever warlord happened to be ruling the area) sent people to conscript soldiers. I was caught. . . .

I was in the army a year. I never did fight any Japanese and by then the Liberation War had started. I didn't know what it was about at that time, but when our regiment came up against the PLA our whole company went over to their side. We didn't want to fight anyway, and why should we fight people like ourselves? That was how I was liberated and able to get back home.

Things soon began to change. We landless labourers all got land in the land reform. Then the Party showed us how to start mutual-aid teams and cooperatives . . . well, you can see yourself how well we live now. Now we are all liberated. Youngsters today can hardly understand what we mean when we talk of starvation in the old times. Everyone in Upper Felicity will eat meat this Spring Festival. Everyone will have new clothes. When I recall the old days, how can I not follow the Party?

From Jack Chen, *A Year in Upper Felicity*, Harrap, 1973.

1 In your own words, list the injustices and hardships of peasants' lives before Liberation, as described by Hsi-Kun.
2 How did the lives of peasants in Upper Felicity change as a result of Liberation?
3 Sources A and B are both reminiscences recorded many years after Liberation. Does this affect their value as historical evidence in any way? Explain your answer.

By the mid-1950s the rule of the Communist Party in China was well-established, and many of the abuses of pre-Liberation society had been abolished. The leaders of the Communist Party, however, disagreed over the future development of the country. Mao Zedong and his supporters wanted a complete break with the past by abolishing all remaining forms of capitalism in order to allow the full development of socialism. At the other extreme, Liu Shaoqi and his supporters favoured a more gradual development of the economy along Soviet Russian lines. The different approaches of the leaders towards China's future development were reflected in a joke that went round the dinner tables at a banquet for Shanghai's leading businessmen in December 1955:

C Mao Zedong asked his two senior colleagues, Liu Shaoqi and Zhou Enlai, how they would make a cat eat a pepper.

'That's easy,' Liu replied, 'You get somebody to hold the cat, stuff the pepper into its mouth, and push it down with a chopstick.'

'No, no,' Mao raised his hands in horror, 'Never use force, that is undemocratic. Everything must be voluntary. How would you do it?' he asked, turning towards Zhou.

'I would starve the cat,' replied the Premier, 'Then I would wrap the pepper in a slice of meat. If the cat is hungry enough he will swallow it whole.'

But Mao still shook his head. 'One must not use deceit either,' he declared. 'Never fool the people.' The other two looked questioningly at him. What would he do?

'It's so easy,' Mao explained. 'Rub the pepper thoroughly into the cat's arse. When it begins to burn, the cat will lick it off – and be happy that it is allowed to do so.'

Quoted in Dick Wilson, *Mao: The People's Emperor*, Hutchinson, 1979.

1 Describe the characters of Mao, Liu and Zhou as they appear in this joke.
2 In general, what uses can historians make of jokes told at the time which they are studying? How reliably can jokes be used for this purpose?
3 Do you consider the joke in source C as reliable evidence of the ways in which people thought about their leaders in 1955? Explain your answer.

Mao Zedong won the argument about the future development of the Chinese economy. In 1958 he announced that China would shortly make a 'Great Leap Forward'. A Five-Year Plan, running from 1958 to 1963, would make China into one of the world's leading industrial nations at the same time as massively boosting her agricultural output. The key to achieving this was the reorganisation of around 700 million Chinese people into Communes, each consisting of some 5000 families. Divided into work brigades and then into work teams, the people of the communes would force the Chinese economy to make great leaps along the road to socialism. One way in which Mao expected this to happen was through a 'backyard steel campaign' in which commune members would increase China's steel output by making iron and steel in small, home-made furnaces. The backyard steel campaign is described in source D by a member of a work brigade in Long Bow village, in conversation with an American writer who visited the village in 1980:

D Two to three thousand people gathered . . . from many different communities. They came with horsecarts, baskets and carrying poles. The smelting started with two or three furnaces. Later we built so many that we lost track of the number. At first we built them with brick from the ground up, but later we dug them as caves. . . . Either way, the overall shape of the furnaces was the same – squat and round. We filled them with coal and ore in alternate layers. We launched a big contest to see who could make the most iron in one day. . . . That whole place turned into one big iron smelter. Smoke billowed down the valley. When we needed fuel we just went to the mine and hauled away whatever coal we saw. . . .

In those days it was easy to get people to come out and work. Nobody worried at all about their livelihood. They didn't care where the next meal was coming from. They just marched off. I went to Tiensheng. My wife went to Shihhui. We just locked our door and took off. Were we afraid of losing anything? No! Who wants anything from anyone else anyway? In those days nobody thought of taking anything. Starting in 1958 people paid little attention to private property. They just went wherever they were sent and didn't worry about anything in the world.

We combined work and military training. All militia members trained every morning. We were all young people. We kept our rifles at the worksite. When the bugle blew for practice we all assembled at once.

Those were great days! Great days!

Soon it was impossible to count the people that overflowed the worksite. The villages all emptied out because all the people went to make iron.

City people came out in busloads from middle schools, primary schools and offices. The schoolchildren carried ore in their kerchiefs or they stuffed their pockets full. The cooks who came with them set up their pots and fires beside the road. . . .

Every time I recall those days I am filled with happiness.

From William Hinton, *Shenfan*, Secker and Warburg, 1983.

Despite the enthusiasm and hard work of the Chinese, the backyard steel campaign failed. Although the backyard furnaces produced colossal amounts of iron, most of it was too impure for industrial use and had to be thrown away. So many furnaces were built that eventually one person in ten was involved in making steel; and this took away so many people from the fields that food production dropped alarmingly. With a famine already gripping large areas of the country, Mao Zedong admitted in 1959 that the Great Leap Forward had failed, saying: 'The chaos caused was on a grand scale, and I take responsibility.'

---

1 What evidence is there in source D to confirm Mao's statement that the Great Leap Forward caused chaos?

2 According to source D, how much popular support was there for the Great Leap Forward?

3 Why do you think the speaker in source D was 'filled with happiness' every time he recalled the days of the Great Leap Forward?

Following the Great Leap Forward disaster, Mao Zedong gave up his post as Head of State to the more moderate Liu Shaoqi, and took a back seat in the day-to-day administration of China. Although Liu and his moderate colleagues hastily reversed many of Mao Zedong's reforms, Mao did not lose his influence over the nation's affairs. As Party Chairman he still had great influence over the mass of Party members. He used that influence in 1966 to start a new political revolution aimed at getting rid of moderates in both the Party and the government.

The Cultural Revolution, as Mao called this anti-moderate campaign, began among school and college students in Beijing who formed groups known as Red Guards. Source E gives us one view of what being a Red Guard entailed. The speaker is Lu Hong, who was seventeen years old at the start of the Cultural Revolution, and who recalled some of her experiences in conversation over dinner with an American journalist in 1979.

E 'I was very young when the Cultural Revolution began,' she told me. . . . 'My schoolmates and I were among the first in Peking* to become Red Guards, we believed deeply in Chairman Mao. I could recite the entire book of the Chairman's quotations backward and forward, we spent hours just shouting the slogans at our teachers.'

Beijing

Hong remembered in particular a winter day, with the temperature below freezing, when she and her faction of Red Guards put on their red armbands and made three of the teachers from their high school kneel on the ground outside without their coats or gloves. 'We had gone to their houses to conduct an investigation, to search them, and we found some English-language books. They were probably only textbooks, but to us it was proof they were worshipping foreign things and were slaves to the foreigners. We held a bonfire and burned everything we had found.' . . .

Two years later, Hong went on, she was one of the first to volunteer when Mao proclaimed, 'It is very necessary for educated young people to go to the countryside to be re-educated by the poor and lower-middle peasants.'

'They put me on a train to the north-east. There were 2400 other high school students in the cars. We were travelling for four. days and didn't know what our destination was until they let us off at a state farm near the Soviet border. At the time, I was full of patriotism and wanted to protect the motherland.

'Then they put us in a dormitory made of mud, with mud walls and mud floors,' she continued. Sixty people slept in one room on two *kangs* made of mud, straw, and manure.' (A *kang* is a raised platform heated by flues running underneath which northern Chinese use for sitting on during the day and sleeping on at night to keep warm.) 'At night, if you came in late, all you could see were sixty heads sticking out of the covers, down a narrow aisle.'

The only way for her to bathe, Hong said, was in a small enamel basin. In the entire eight years she spent on the farm, she never got to take a bath or shower.

But the worst problem was boredom. The nearest town was a three hour walk. That was where she had to go to see a movie. But in the first five years on the farm, she saw only three movies, all of which she had seen before in Peking. There were no books or magazines for sale, and many of her friends had not brought any with them.

'After getting up at five a.m. to work in the fields, you were too tired to read at night anyway, so some of the young people forgot how to read and write.'

Still, Hong was lucky. Her father was a cadre* and eventually arranged through the back door to get her transferred back to Peking.

a Party official

'I spent eight years fanning the flames of revolution; it was like losing a big chunk out of your life. Now I would like to contribute to the motherland, but what do I have? I never finished high school. It's like my friends say, the Chinese people don't live, they just exist.'

From Fox Butterfield, *China: Alive in the Bitter Sea*, Hodder and Stoughton, 1982.

Source F gives us a very different picture of what it meant to be a Red Guard. It is an extract from a Chinese news magazine published for English readers in the 1970s.

F In the virgin forests of the Greater Khingan Mountains in Heilungkiang Province, a team made up of educated young women is engaged in building bridges. They are former Red Guards hailing from Shanghai, Kiamusze and other cities, who came to the frontier region in 1969 in response to the great teaching of Chairman Mao, **'Young people should face the world, brave the storm and temper themselves in struggle to become successors to the**

revolutionary cause of the proletariat.' There, out in the wilds, led and helped by the worker-People's Liberation Army Mao Tsetung* Thought propaganda team, they build bridges for the revolution.

* Mao Zedong

They never stop work, whether in summer when it rains for days on end or in the severe cold of 50°C below zero. Once the members of the re-inforcing rods group were high up wiring the rods together when a wet snow began to fall. The veteran workers were concerned on seeing that their clothes were thoroughly drenched and tried to persuade them to go down. But they answered firmly, 'If we're not tempered in wind and rain, how can we learn to wage revolution! The greater the difficulties and dangers, the harder we should press forward!'

And so the women bridge-builders steeled their revolutionary will and remoulded their thinking as they learned technique. In about six months, they successfully built a 110-metre-long, 5-metre-wide, 5-arch reinforced concrete highway-bridge.

Anon.

---

1 How does source F (a) agree with, and (b) disagree with the view of Red Guards in source E?
2 According to source E, how enthusiastic was Lu Hong about her Red Guard activities when she first became a Red Guard? How did her feelings change after eight years working in the country?
3 Judging by sources E and F, what were the Red Guards' motives for taking part in the Cultural Revolution? Quote from the sources to illustrate each of the motives you suggest.

The Cultural Revolution did not solve the arguments between moderates and radicals in the Chinese Communist Party. The early 1970s saw increasingly bitter debates between them over which road China should follow towards socialism. The moderates wanted to concentrate on China's economic development, while the radicals demanded a period of class struggle to get rid of the remaining conservative and bourgeois elements in Chinese society. A radical campaign known as 'Pi Lin, Pi Kung'* aimed to achieve this in 1974. Lin Biao, the disgraced PLA leader who had died in mysterious circumstances in 1971, was attacked alongside the ancient Chinese philosopher Confucius for wanting the return of capitalism. Source G is an example of the methods used by radicals in the 'Pi Lin, Pi Kung' campaign; it is an extract from an English language textbook published for Chinese schoolchildren in 1975. It is important to note that the textbook from which it comes was a standard textbook approved by the government Ministry of Education and used in schools throughout China.

Criticise Lin, Criticise Confucius

G CARRY THE STRUGGLE TO CRITICISE LIN BIAO AND CONFUCIUS THROUGH TO THE END

Lin Biao and Confucius were jackals of the same lair. Confucius wanted to restore the slave-owning system and Lin Biao wanted to restore capitalism. They sang the same tune and took the same road.

Lin Biao was an out-and-out disciple of Confucius. He tried to change the Party's basic line and turn back the wheel of history. We will never allow this to happen.

The criticism of Lin Biao and Confucius is a serious class struggle and a political and ideological struggle in the superstructure. We must answer Chairman Mao's call and carry the struggle to criticise Lin Biao and Confucius through to the end.

New Words and Expressions
1. Jackal ['dzækc:l] n.   2. lair [lɛa] n.   3. want [wont] vt.
4. restore [ris'to] vt.   5. slave-owning ['sleiv' ouning] a.
6. system ['sistim] n.   7. capitalism ['kæpitelizam] n.   8. sing
[sing] vt ... 9. tune [tju:n] 10. out-and-out [auten'aut] a.
11. disciple [di'saipl] n. 12. basic ['beisik] a. 13. line [lain] n.
14. wheel [hwi:l] 15. allow [e'lau] vt. 16. criticism ['kritisizem]
17. serious ['siəriəs] a.   18. ideological [aidie' lodzikel]
19. superstructure ['sju:perstruktje] n.

From *English*, Ministry of Education of the People's Republic of China, 1975.

1 What do you think was the aim of the Ministry of Education in including this material in a school textbook?
2 Judging by words that do not appear in the list of 'New Words and Expressions', what political terms used in the passage did Chinese school students already understand?
3 Why would many people in other countries disapprove of using this material in a school textbook?
4 Judging by what you have read about the Cultural Revolution, what dangers are there in encouraging students to take part in a political campaign like this?

In the power struggle between moderates and radicals that took place in the mid-1970s, the radicals were wiped out as a political force. The victory of the moderates could clearly be seen in a Communist Party document of 1981, entitled 'Resolution on Certain Questions of Party History'.

H The Cultural Revolution, which lasted from May 1966 to October 1976, was responsible for the most severe setback and the heaviest losses suffered by the Party since the founding of the People's Republic. It was initiated and led by Comrade Mao Zedong. . . . The erroneous 'left' theses on which he based himself . . . conformed neither to Marxism-Leninism nor to Chinese reality . . .

The Cultural Revolution did not in fact constitute a revolution or social progress in any sense, nor could it possibly have done so. [It] . . . brought catastrophe to the Party, the state and the whole people.

Quoted in Philip Short, *The Dragon and the Bear: Inside China and Russia Today*, Hodder and Stoughton, 1982.

Using sources A to H in this chapter as evidence:
1 List the ways in which the Chinese people have achieved 'liberation' under Communist rule since 1949.
2 Describe the disadvantages of Communist rule that have accompanied 'liberation'.

18 Conflict in the Middle East: the Arab-Israeli conflict since 1917

In 1917, after five hundred years of rule over the peoples of the Middle East, the Turkish Empire was approaching extinction. Defeat in the First World War, and a revolt of the Arab peoples of the Empire, had dealt mortal blows to an already feeble 'sick man of Europe', as European statesmen liked to call it. As the hour of its death approached, all those who stood to gain from the end of the Turkish Empire gathered for a division of the spoils: foreign governments arranged to partition it among themselves; oil companies made plans to drill for oil beneath its sands; Arab nationalists prepared to set up their own governments in independent national states; and Zionist Jews got ready to settle in the Holy Land of Palestine from which Jews had been expelled in ancient times.

The Turkish Empire finally collapsed in 1922. Ever since, the area of the Middle East which it once ruled has been convulsed by revolts, wars, massacres, and calamities of all kinds. And of all the causes for dispute, the greatest difficulties have arisen from the creation of a Jewish nation, Israel, in one small province of the former Empire – Palestine. The sources in this chapter show some of the reasons why the creation and existence of Israel have contributed to major conflicts in the Middle East, and why those conflicts show no sign of being resolved in the twentieth century.

Although nobody knew it at the time, the behaviour of the British government in 1917 was to be a major cause of conflict in the Middle East for years to come. In an attempt to undermine the Turkish Empire during the First World War, the British government authorised Colonel T. E. Lawrence – 'Lawrence of Arabia' – to promise independent kingdoms to Emir Feisel and Emir Hussein in return for fighting their Turkish overlords. At the same time the British government promised the Jews of the World Zionist Federation* a 'national home' for Jewish people in Palestine. The promise was contained in this letter:

an organisation set up in 1897 to campaign for the settlement of Jews in Palestine, from which the Romans expelled them in the first century AD, and which many Jews regarded as their ancient and rightful homeland

A

Foreign Office,
November 2nd 1917

Dear Lord Rothschild,

I have much pleasure in conveying to you, on behalf of His Majesty's Government, the following declaration of sympathy with Jewish Zionist aspirations which has been submitted to, and approved by, the Cabinet.

'His Majesty's Government view with favour the establishment in Palestine of a national home for the Jewish people, and will use their best endeavours to facilitate the achievement of this object, it being clearly understood that nothing shall be done which may prejudice the civil and religious rights of existing non-Jewish communities in Palestine, or the rights and political status enjoyed by Jews in any other country.'

I should be grateful if you would bring this declaration to the knowledge of the Zionist Federation.

Yours sincerely,
Arthur Balfour.

Original letter deposited by Lord Rothschild in The British Museum: Additional Manuscripts, 41 178 folios 1 and 3.

1 Suggest what the term 'national home' means. How does it differ from the term 'nation'?
2 (a) What are 'civil and religious rights'?
  (b) Which civil and religious rights belonging to 'non-Jewish communities' in Palestine do you think the Cabinet had in mind when making this declaration?
  (c) How might these rights be threatened by the establishment of a 'national home' for Jews in Palestine?
3 One Arab complaint about the Balfour Declaration was that it called the Arabs in Palestine 'non-Jewish communities'. Why do you think they objected to this?
4 A wit said in 1917 that Arthur Balfour had promised the Promised Land to more than one people. What do you think he meant?

Many Arabs were alarmed by the Balfour Declaration, as Balfour's letter to Lord Rothschild became known. The objections of Arabs to it can clearly be seen in this statement issued by the General Syrian Congress in 1919:

B We oppose the pretensions of the Zionists to create a Jewish commonwealth in the southern part of Syria, known as Palestine, and oppose Zionist migration to any part of our country; for we do not acknowledge their title but consider them a grave peril to our people from the national, economic and political points of view. Our Jewish compatriots shall enjoy common rights and assume the common responsibilities.

We ask that there should be no separation of the southern part of Syria, known as Palestine, nor of the coastal western zone, which includes Lebanon, from the Syrian country. We desire that the unity of the country should be guaranteed against partition under whatever circumstances.

From a *Memorandum Presented to the King-Crane Commission by the General Syrian Congress*, 2 July 1919. Quoted in Walter Laqueur and Barry Rubin (eds), *The Israel-Arab Reader, A Documentary History of the Middle East Conflict*, Penguin, 1976.

1 According to source B, to whom did Palestine belong in 1919?
2 Judging by source B, what would Jews (a) be allowed, and (b) not be allowed in an Arab-controlled Palestine?
3 How does source B suggest that the promises made in the Balfour Declaration (source A) would be difficult for the British government to keep?

The British government had to live with the consequences of the Balfour Declaration, for in 1920 the League of Nations made Palestine a mandated territory under British supervision. This meant that Britain would govern Palestine until it considered the Palestinians capable of governing themselves. Under the terms of the mandate, a Jewish Agency was set up to help create the 'National Home' that Balfour had promised. Led by a Zionist, Chaim Weizmann, the Jewish Agency arranged the immigration of increasing numbers of Jews into Palestine during the 1920s. By 1929 there were over 150,000 Jews living in Palestine, twice the number living there in 1920. Many of the immigrants set up co-operative farms known as kibbutzim. The photograph in source C shows one group of Jewish settlers working on a kibbutz in 1929:

C

> 1 What impression does the photograph create of (a) the kibbutz, and (b) the workers?
> 2 For what purposes could (a) a Zionist, and (b) an anti-Zionist have used this photograph?

The 600,000 Arabs living in Palestine had not originally been anti-Jewish, but by 1929 they were feeling threatened by the growing numbers of Jewish settlers there. Arab annoyance burst out in riots in 1929 in which over a hundred people were killed. Hostility to Jewish immigration increased during the 1930s when the rate of immigration climbed sharply as Jews left Germany to escape Nazi persecution. Riots broke out again in 1933, this time against the British as well as the Jews. Unrest turned into a major Arab revolt in 1936–37. The British used 20,000 troops to put down the revolt, and started a series of government enquiries into the problems caused by large-scale Jewish immigration. In 1939 a British government White Paper made a number of recommendations about the situation, including the following:

D Section 4. It is not part of the [British] Government's policy that Palestine should become a Jewish state. They would indeed regard it as contrary to their obligations to the Arabs under the mandate. Section 10. It is proposed to establish within ten years 'an independent Palestine State ... in which Jews and Arabs combine in government in such a way as to ensure that the essential interests of each community are safeguarded.'

Section 14. (1) For each of the next five years a quota of 10,000 Jewish immigrants will be allowed . . . (apart from a special quota in the near future of 25,000 refugees) 'as a special contribution towards the Jewish refugee problem. . . .' (3) After the period of five years no further Jewish immigration will be permitted unless the Arabs of Palestine are prepared to acquiesce in it.

From *Palestine Statement of Policy,* Cmd. 6019, HMSO, 1939.

1 How does section 4 of the White Paper seem to contradict the Balfour Declaration (source A)?
2 Why do you think the British government thought that a special immigration quota of 25,000 would be needed for Jews 'in the near future'?
3 What criticisms might (a) Arabs, and (b) Jews have made of the White Paper? Which of them do you think were most likely to be unhappy about it? Explain your answer.

The 1939 White Paper settled nothing. Extreme Zionists, appalled at the attitude of the British, formed terrorist groups to drive them out of Palestine. Moderate Zionists campaigned vigorously for unlimited Jewish immigration. Neighbouring Arab states formed an Arab League and warned that the creation of a joint Arab-Jewish Palestine State was entirely unacceptable.

Faced with such opposition, the British found it increasingly difficult to govern Palestine. This photograph of central Jerusalem in 1946 illustrates some of those difficulties. Nicknamed 'Bevingrad' by local Jews after Ernest Bevin, the British Foreign Secretary, this was one of several heavily defended security areas in the Holy City.

E

What does this photograph reveal about
1 the difficulties the British faced in governing Palestine?
2 the effects of the conflict in Palestine on everyday life in Jerusalem?

In 1947 the British government washed its hands of Palestine and handed over its responsibilities to the United Nations Organisation. The UNO tried to solve the Palestine problem by partitioning the country into separate Arab and Jewish states. The reactions of Jews and Arabs to the UNO plan differed sharply. Jews danced and celebrated in the streets while Arabs warned grimly that the creation of a Jewish state would lead to war. The Jewish viewpoint can be seen in the Proclamation of Independence of the State of Israel, issued on 14 May 1948:

F The land of Israel was the birthplace of the Jewish people. Here their spiritual, religious and national identity was formed. Here they achieved independence and created a culture of national and universal significance. Here they wrote and gave the Bible to the world.

Exiled from the land of Israel the Jewish people remained faithful to it in all the countries of their dispersion, never ceasing to pray or hope for their return and the restoration of their national freedom.

Impelled by this historic association, Jews strove throughout the centuries to go back to the land of their fathers and regain their statehood. In recent decades they returned in their masses. They reclaimed the wilderness, revived their language, built cities and villages, and established a vigorous and ever-growing community, with its own economic and cultural life. . . .

It is the natural right of the Jewish people to lead, as do other nations, an independent existence in its sovereign state.

ACCORDINGLY WE, the members of the National Council, representing the Jewish people in Palestine and the World Zionist Movement . . . HEREBY PROCLAIM the establishment of the Jewish State in Palestine, to be called *Medinath Yisrael* (The State of Israel) . . .

THE STATE OF ISRAEL will be open to the immigration of Jews from all countries of their dispersion; will promote the development of the country for the benefit of all its inhabitants; will be based on the principles of liberty, justice and peace as conceived by the Prophets of Israel; will uphold the full social and political equality of all its citizens, without distinction of religion, race or sex; will guarantee freedom of religion, conscience, education and culture; will safeguard the Holy Places of all religions; and will loyally uphold the principles of the United Nations Charter. . . .

From Walter Laqueur (ed.), *The Israel-Arab Reader: A Documentary History of the Middle East Conflict*, Weidenfeld and Nicolson, 1969.

---

1 In your own words, explain how the Proclamation justifies the creation of a Jewish state in Palestine.

2 Which aspects of the Proclamation do you think Arabs most disliked? Explain your answer.

One Arab response to the Proclamation of the State of Israel came from Abdur Rahman Azzam Pasha, Secretary-General of the Arab

League, predicting at a Cairo Press Conference on 15 May 1948 that war must inevitably follow:

G This will be a war of extermination and a momentous massacre which will be spoken of like the Mongolian massacres and the Crusades.

Quoted in Christopher Sykes, *Crossroads to Israel*, Collins, 1965.

Most people expected the Jews to lose the war which followed, in which 20,000 Israeli troops faced over 30,000 Arab troops attacking from several fronts to support the Arab Liberation Army of Palestinians. Against all the odds, however, the Israelis defeated the Arab armies and doubled the size of Israel.

The war of 1947–48 magnified a problem that had already begun to develop in 1947 – the migration of Palestinian Arabs to the neighbouring Arab states of Lebanon, Syria, Iraq, Jordan and Egypt. Fearing reprisals from the victorious Israelis, some 750,000 Arabs fled from their homes to live in makeshift refugee camps across the border from Israel. Neither Israel nor the Arab states were willing to make permanent arrangements for the settlement of the refugees, so they and their descendants were forced to remain in the camps, living in extreme poverty as stateless and unwelcome aliens.

Some of the Palestinian refugees became *fedayeen*, freedom fighters using terrorist methods to fight Israel. Almost as soon as the 1947–48 war was over, cross-border terrorist attacks against Israeli targets began. In response to over 11,000 raids by *fedayeen* in the years 1949–56, the Israelis hit back with massive reprisals against the Arab states in which the refugees lived. This in turn led the *fedayeen* to use ever more extreme tactics against Israel. The extent of their feelings can be judged from this statement issued in 1964 by Al Fatah, the Palestine Liberation Movement, in reply to Arabs who suggested that extreme tactics would only invite more Israeli reprisals:

H We announce to the whole world that we shall launch our revolution with sticks and knives, with old revolvers and crooked hunting rifles, in order to teach a lesson to those who suffer from nightmares about Israeli tanks and planes. Everybody says that Israel will blow up Gaza*, massacre the Palestinians, invade the Arab countries. Israel. Israel. Israel. But nobody considers what we can do – how we shall burn citrus plantations, demolish factories, blow up bridges, and cut off oil communication lines. The revolution will last a year, two years and more, up to twenty or thirty years. As a matter of fact, let the Zionists conquer the West Bank, blow up Gaza and massacre our population. Let the American Sixth Fleet make a move. The Arab people will stand as a dam to help the revolution. History has never witnessed the failure of a popular revolution.

* one of the main areas of refugee camps

Quoted in John Laffin, *Fedayeen: The Arab-Israeli Dilemma*, Cassell, 1973.

---

1 How can you tell from source H that the *fedayeen* were often poorly armed in the 1960s?
2 Judging by source H, why did Al Fatah believe that they would succeed in liberating Palestine, despite being poorly armed?

Neither Al Fatah nor any of the other liberation groups that mush-
roomed in the refugee camps during the 1960s succeeded in liberating
Palestine from the Israelis. By the 1980s, several generations of
Palestinians had grown up in the refugee camps, knowing about
Palestine only what their parents and teachers could tell them. Source
I shows one of the ways in which young Palestinians viewed their
distant homeland: it is a calendar made by a child in a school in a
refugee camp in Jordan. The Arabic words for 'Palestine' and 'We
shall return' stand out above a poem urging Palestinians to fight a war
of revenge against Israel.

---

1 What points do you think the pupil was trying to make by drawing (a) a soldier, (b) a mosque,
  (c) Jordanian flags on the calendar?
2 What does this calendar tell you about the attitudes of young Palestinians towards Israel in the
  1980s?

By 1980 the strongest branches of the Palestinian Liberation Organisation were in Lebanon, where a civil war had disrupted the country since 1975. Taking advantage of the chaos caused by the civil war, the PLO had built itself up as a formidable military and political force in the capital, Beirut, where thousands of Palestinian refugees lived in sprawling camps. In 1982 Israel felt so threatened by the activities of the PLO in Beirut that it carried out a full-scale invasion of Lebanon in order to deal with them. With the help of their Christian Phalangist allies in Lebanon, the Israelis forced the PLO to withdraw completely from Beirut. With the PLO gone the Phalangists were able to enter the refugee camps in Beirut to settle old scores with the Arabs who had sheltered the PLO. Encouraged by Israeli troops, the Phalangists massacred many hundreds of Arabs in the Sabra-Chatila camp between 16 and 18 September 1982. Shortly after the massacre, a survivor named Jamal described some of the things he saw to Caroline Tisdall, a British journalist in Beirut:

J That night the entire southern entrance [to the camp] was bulldozed. We heard the noise of the engines working and thought they were tanks. That's where the Makdaad family were killed. I was sure then that the entire east side of the camp was empty of people. They killed everyone they found, but the point is the way they killed them. They found a mother holding a five-year old. They took the child and pretended they were about to kill him, not just once but two or three times. Then they killed him and told her he would have been a *fedayeen* one day. They said 'We don't need to kill you – you'll die with this memory.' There was Fahd, an 18-year-old Syrian whose head was split open with an axe in front of his mother. There was Abu Brahim who survived – he was one of the fighters, but he lives with the memory that his mother, sister and brothers were killed and that his pregnant wife had the baby cut out of her and was then killed. They must have been crazed to do things like that. After the massacre we found the place where some of them had stayed in that night, among the breeze blocks we had brought for rebuilding. Piles of lager cans, and two syringes. . . .

We do not know how many died. The Red Cross said 1500 at the time, and then there were at least 900 who were driven off and never seen again. Some dead bodies were found along the roads going east and to the mountains.

You can't separate the war and the massacre. I believe they were trying to set an example for the other Arab countries, to prevent the other Arab peoples ever accepting the Palestinian forces as an organised force in their midst, and to show them what would happen if they did.

From Selim Nassib with Caroline Tisdall, *Beirut: Frontline Story*, Pluto Press, 1983.

---

1 Why did the Phalangists kill the five-year-old boy but not his mother?

2 For what other reasons, according to Jamal, did the Phalangists behave with such cruelty?

To many people not living in the Middle East, the complex and long-drawn-out civil war in Lebanon seemed almost impossible to understand. According to David Hirst, a British journalist writing in the *Guardian* in 1985, not even the fighters in the civil war entirely understood it:

K Last month, *Al-Shira'a*, a weekly magazine*, sent a reporter to talk to the ordinary militiamen of predominantly Muslim West Beirut. She put a series of set questions.   * pro-Arab and pro-Muslim

'Why are you fighting?' she asked Ziyad, a 20-year-old militiaman of six years standing. 'Against the Fascist, isolationist collaborators with Israel.' And what does 'Fascist' mean? 'It means Nazism.' And what does 'Nazism' mean? 'I don't know.'

Abu Rabi, a 22-year-old, took up arms six years ago. 'To fight the enemies.' And who were they? 'The enemies of religion.' Religion in what sense? 'The Islamic religion. But not in defence of a sect – I am not a fanatic.' Do you want Islamic government in Lebanon? 'Yes, as in the days of the Prophet, praise be upon him.' Do you know the meaning of secularism* ? 'I heard of it. But I don't   * non-religious government
know what it means.' The meaning of democracy? 'No.' Do you know anything about the late President Nasser? 'Nothing at all.' Arab nationalism? 'Nothing.' The partition of Palestine? 'No.' The Balfour Declaration? 'Never heard of it. . . .'   From the *Guardian*, 26 August, 1985.

---

1 Suggest why the militiamen in source K knew so little about the history of the Arab-Israeli conflict.
2 Bearing in mind that this report appeared in a pro-Arab, pro-Muslim magazine, how useful do you consider it as a source of evidence?

---

1 Using sources A to K in this chapter as evidence, list as many reasons as you can to explain why Arabs and Israelis have been in conflict since the 1920s.
2 Which of those causes of conflict seems to you to be the most troublesome? Explain your answer.
3 Many people believe that there will never be peace in the Middle East between Arabs and Israelis. Judging by what you have read in this chapter, why do you think they believe this?

19 A United Kingdom? Great Britain since 1945

In 1945 Great Britain was still at the centre of a mighty empire which straddled a fifth of the globe's land surface in all five continents. And although battered and shaken by six years of total war, Britain was still one of the three great military powers of the world, as well as one of the richest.

By 1953, when Queen Elizabeth II came to the throne, the former British Empire was breaking up. India, Pakistan and Burma had already won their independence, while nationalists in Africa and the West Indies were preparing to struggle for theirs. Nevertheless, Britain's future in 1953 still seemed bright.

One newspaper writer described the situation in 1953 like this:

A 1953. No unemployment to speak of, a national health service and social security system to soften the old class warfare, a new and fairer educational system, an expanding industrial base, a lead in nuclear technology, a place at the head of a great commonwealth. A new Golden Age!

Quoted in David Robins, *We Hate Humans*, Penguin, 1984.

And the young Queen Elizabeth herself said, on being crowned:

B I am sure that this, my Coronation, is not the symbol of a power and splendour that are gone but a declaration of our hopes for the future.

Quoted in Christopher Brooker, *The Neophiliacs*, Fontana/Collins, 1969.

There were, however, major problems already looming on the horizon. The first concerned the inhabitants of the former territories of Britain's shrinking empire. Encouraged to emigrate to Britain during a labour shortage in the 1950s, large numbers of invited immigrants, most of them black, arrived in the major towns and cities. Almost immediately, resentment of the newcomers built up among the people already living and working there. At first, this resentment was disguised. As a West Indian worker in Liverpool put it in 1951:

C In America you know where you stand; in England people say they have no prejudice or colour bar, but in practice we know that it is there. But because it is not out in the open we cannot fight it. In America you can either avoid trouble, or you know where to go, and what to do, if you want to fight against it.

From Anthony H. Richmond, *Colour Prejudice in Britain: A Study of West Indian Workers in Liverpool, 1941–1951*, Routledge and Kegan Paul, 1954.

As time went by, and as the numbers of black Britons increased, the hostility of some white people became more open. In areas such as Brixton in South London, where many black people lived, that hostility often seemed most noticeable among the police. Joseph Hunte, a

West Indian lawyer, investigated complaints about police behaviour in Brixton in the early 1960s. Source D is an extract from his findings:

D In 1963 a number of policemen entered No. 33 Lambert Road, Brixton, where it was alleged that a party was being held. The police knocked on the door of each room. A West Indian who lived in the top flat was aroused from his sleep. The police entered and requested to search his room. The man was in his pyjamas. The story was that the man asked for a search warrant of the police, and one of the policemen replied, 'Yes, here it is,' whereupon a fist blow landed on the jaw of the man. The blow was the warrant. . . .

In December 1964, a peaceful party leaving for home during a dance at the Lambeth Town Hall was set upon by police and their dogs. The members of the party were humiliated, threatened, assaulted and otherwise manhandled. The writer was a witness to this episode. . . .

Eye-witnesses to an incident at Coldharbour Lane last year revealed that when a West Indian sought assistance from two police constables, after his car was involved in an accident, one of the constables asked the West Indian, 'What do you black bastard want?' This brought about an exchange of words as to the abruptness of the police officers. The result of this was that the constables took the West Indian to the police station by dragging him along the road, beat him up at the police station and charged him for assault. . . .

Two cases have been brought to my notice which involved policemen in Brixton deliberately stopping cars which contained both coloured men and white girls and brought them in – one for driving under the influence of drinks and the other for using a woman for immoral purposes.

Many more cases could be brought in to show that the police have been in some measure vindictive towards the West Indian community when the situation does not warrant it. . . .

Quoted in Frank Field and Patricia Hakin (eds.), *Black Britons*, Oxford University Press, 1971.

---

1 On what evidence did Joseph Hunte base his allegations in source D? Do you have any reason to doubt the reliability of that evidence?
2 What do you think the West Indian worker in source C meant by 'colour bar'? To what extent does source D support his opinion that there was an unofficial colour bar in England?

Because most immigrants settled in the industrial cities of Great Britain, especially the crowded 'inner city' areas, government planners found themselves confronted with major problems in providing for their needs. Source E shows one example of those problems. It is an extract from a report by the Inner London Education Authority called 'Improving Secondary Schools', published in 1984:

E Pupils whose mother tongue is not English have been a significant minority in London's schools since the service* was founded. . . . In the last two years, however, for a variety of reasons, there has been a nine per cent increase in pupils speaking English as a second language so that in 1983 one in six children in the ILEA came within this category. . . . A recent census discovered that 147 languages are spoken in London schools, in some cases by large numbers, in others by a scatter of sometimes isolated pupils. The languages represented most frequently in schools at present are Bengali, Turkish, Gujerati, Spanish, Greek, Urdu, Punjabi, Chinese, Italian, Arabic, French and Portuguese. Some pupils are fully bilingual; some have an insecure command of English; while a few speak none at all. . . . The Authority has responded by appointing its first inspector for bilingualism/community and heritage languages.'

the Inner London Education Authority

From *Improving Secondary Schools, Report of the Committee on the Curriculum and Organisation of Secondary Schools*, ILEA, 1984.

---

1 What problems may arise from the multiplicity of languages spoken in London's schools for (a) the pupils speaking those languages, (b) their teachers, and (c) the administrators of the ILEA?
2 How do you explain the fact that so many different languages are spoken in London schools?

Dislike and resentment of non-white minorities led from the 1950s onwards to the growth of racist groups such as the National Front, whose main aim was to force immigrants to leave Britain. A member of the National Front described his views in an interview with a sociologist in 1977:

F I don't want to be with black people, I don't want a multi-racial country. Why should I? I've got nothing in common with them, they don't want to mix with me any more than I do with them. Why should I be forced to live with them? I want to be able to go into a pub, I want to be able to go to work without seeing a black face. The National Front is saying the sort of things I want to hear. I wouldn't be cruel. If I ran over a black in my car, I wouldn't just leave him lying in the road; I'd kick him into the gutter. I don't want them here. I want them to leave. I understand that this might be a bit disruptive. If the barricades do go up, it won't be the middle class on one side and the working class on the other; it'll be white on one side and black on the other, with just a few race traitors on their side. I want to be with just our own. I don't want to live in a system that falls over itself to favour blacks. If there's anything going on in this country, I want it for myself.

From Jeremy Seabrook, *What Went Wrong: Working People and the Ideals of the Labour Movement*, Gollancz, 1978.

---

1 What do you think the speaker in source F means by saying that it 'might be a bit disruptive' if black people were made to leave Britain?
2 How do you explain the prejudices shown by the speaker in source F?

The problems of Britain's 'inner cities' flared up in the early 1980s in outbreaks of rioting which devastated inner city areas in Bristol, London, Liverpool and Birmingham. In a government enquiry into the causes of the Brixton riots in London in 1981, Lord Scarman wrote:

G The evidence which I have received . . . leaves no doubt in my mind that racial disadvantage is a fact of current British life. It was, I am equally sure, a significant factor in the causation of the Brixton disorders. Urgent action is needed if it is not to become an endemic, ineradicable disease threatening the very survival of our society. . . . 'Institutional racism' does not exist in Britain: but racial disadvantage and its nasty associate, racial discrimination, have not yet been eliminated. They poison minds and attitudes: they are, and so long as they remain will continue to be, a potent factor of unrest.

The role of the police has to be considered against this background. . . . The police do not create social deprivation or racial disadvantage: they are not responsible for the disadvantages of the ethnic minorities. Yet their role is critical. . . . If they neglect consultation and cooperation with the local community, unrest is certain and riot becomes probable.

On the social front . . . the attack on racial disadvantage must be more direct than it has been. It must be coordinated by central government who, with the local authorities, must ensure that the funds made available are directed to specific areas of racial disadvantage. I have in mind particularly education and unemployment. . . .

From Lord Scarman, *The Scarman Report*, Penguin Books, 1982.

---

1 What does Lord Scarman mean by (a) racism, (b) institutional racism, (c) racial disadvantage, (d) racial discrimination?
2 Why do you think Lord Scarman believed that the survival of British society was threatened by racial disadvantage?
3 What reforms does he suggest are necessary to avoid future unrest?

By the time Lord Scarman wrote his report, riot and unrest of a different kind had been going on for more than twenty years in another part of the Kingdom – Northern Ireland. There, since the start of the 'Ulster Troubles' in 1968–69, riot, murder, arson, kidnap and bombing had become depressingly regular features of British life. By 1985 some 2,500 men, women and children had been killed in the course of the 'Troubles'. Some people argued that the violence would never stop while the British Army remained in Northern Ireland. The argument against withdrawing from Northern Ireland was put by a British Army commander in an interview in 1978:

H I believe very strongly that if we just walk out and say 'Stuff it! Let the police carry on', they just could not operate. That is why we are here. It would be anarchy if we walked out, and a tremendous victory for an illegal organisation. The rule of law must win. We must work by it and obey it. The Army provides the back-up for this and it is, in my view, democracy working. If we walk out, we are forsaking democracy. It is as simple as that.

From Desmond Hamill, *Pig in the Middle: The Army in Northern Ireland, 1969–1985*, Methuen, 1985.

To Republicans in Northern Ireland, however, it was not as simple as that. In many cases they believed that their continued union with Britain was the very opposite of 'democracy working'. This view is reflected in source I, a Christmas card sent out in 1983 by the Irish Republican Army. Above the message 'Happy Christmas to you' is a drawing of policemen in the Royal Ulster Constabulary questioning a family during their Christmas shopping.

From John Chartres, Bert Henshaw, Michael Dewar, *Northern Ireland Scrapbook*, Arms and Armour Press, 1986.

I

1 What impression does the card give of (a) the policemen, (b) the family?

2 What political message do you think the card is trying to put across?

3 How useful is source J as evidence of Republican attitudes in Northern Ireland?

Particularly worrying was the fact that very young people often took a leading part in confrontations with the police and the army. The scale of the problem can be seen in this conversation between Morris Fraser, a child psychiatrist, and three Belfast youngsters in 1972:

J The boy in the green anorak took my pencil and drew two parallel lines on the back of an envelope.

'That's the street, right?'

He added a neat row of dots outside each line, then a rectangle in the middle.

'These are the lamp-posts, and that's the Army Land Rover coming up the street. You tie your cheesewire between two of the lamp-posts about six feet up. There's always a soldier standing in the back of the jeep; even with searchlights, he can't see the wire in the dark. It's just at the right height to catch his throat. Then, when the jeep stops, we can come out and throw stones.'

His friend, two years older, disagreed.

'Only kids throw stones. What we do is fill our pockets with them and carry hurley sticks. If you put a stone on the ground and swing a stick as hard as you can, you can hit a soldier below his shield and cripple him. We once cut a squad of thirty-six down to six in ten minutes like that.'

The third boy supported him.

'Then,' he said, 'we come in with petrol bombs. If a soldier lowers his shield to protect himself against the stones, you can lob a bomb over the top and get him that way.'

From Norris Fraser, *Children in Conflict*, Secker and Warburg, 1972.

---

1 What light does source H throw on the difficulties facing the British Army in Northern Ireland in the 1970s?

2 What does source H tell you about the attitude of some Northern Irish people to the British Army?

For much of the time, people living in mainland Britain were able to ignore the distressing conflict in Northern Ireland. At regular intervals, however, they received unpleasant reminders of it in the form of bomb explosions. Source K shows the results of a car bomb explosion in London in 1975.

K

1 What do you think the IRA hoped to achieve by exploding a bomb in London?
2 What arguments are there against using bombs for this purpose?
3 How might a member of the IRA have defended the use of the bomb in source K?

The troubles in Northern Ireland were not the only conflict that divided the British people after 1945. Increasingly in the 1960s and 1970s, Britain's workplaces were the scene of bitter struggles between trade unionists and their employers. The struggle was most intense while Edward Heath's Conservative government was in power from 1970 to 1974. During those years the National Union of Mineworkers took the lead in organising strikes in pursuit of improved wages. Arthur Scargill, one of the strike organisers of the NUM, and later its President, recalled the aims of the 1972 strike in an interview in 1975:

L You see we took the view that we were in a class war. We were not playing cricket on the village green like they did in '26*. We were out to defeat Heath and Heath's policies because we were fighting a government. Anyone who thinks otherwise was living in cloud-cuckoo land. We had to declare war on them and the only way you could declare war was to attack the vulnerable points. They were the points of *energy*; the power stations, the coke depots, the coal depots, the points of supply. And this is what we did.

Well, the miners' union was not opposed to the distribution of coal. We were only opposed to the distribution of coal to industry because we wished to paralyse the nation's economy. It is as simple as that.

* when the NUM took part in the General Strike.

From *New Left Review*, September 1975.

1 What do you think Arthur Scargill meant by 'a class war'?
2 In what ways are power stations, coke and coal depots, and energy supply points 'the vulnerable points' of a government?
3 Judging by source L, what was the ultimate aim of the 1972 mineworkers' strike?

Some of the ugliest scenes of industrial conflict were seen in London in 1977, when trade unionists formed mass pickets outside the Grunwick photograph processing plant. Their aim was to win a long-running dispute over trade union recognition with the owner of Grunwick by closing down his plant. Their method was to try to prevent workers entering the plant by blocking the entrance. The police, however, had a legal duty to keep the highway clear, and the streets around the Grunwick plant thus became a battlefield as police and pickets struggled for control of the plant's entrances. Sources M and N show two opposite views of the confrontation, in which 297 people were arrested and 97 police were injured, one seriously. Source M is a comment by

Superintendent Hickman-Smith, in charge of the police at Grunwick, speaking to reporters on 13 June 1977:

M Everyone who wanted to go into work was being called a 'scab' and shouted at. There were about 200 people massing outside the gates and we had to put a cordon on to allow free access to the premises. I do not think there was any over-reaction. We were quite impartial. We are put in a situation like this and we have a duty to keep the highway clear and allow peaceful picketing.

From *The Times*, 14 June 1977.

Source: Times Newspapers.

N

1 Does source N support the statement in source M? Explain your answer.
2 What do you think was the aim of the photographer in taking and then publishing the photograph? Does this affect its value as a historical source? Explain your answer.

1 What do you think the writer of source A meant by 'a new golden age'? Why did he believe that Britain in 1953 was entering a new golden age?
2 List the ways in which C to N suggest that Britain since 1953 has not experienced that 'golden age'.
3 Do you think that the author of this book can be accused of bias in his selection of sources for this chapter? If so, suggest how a different picture of Britain since 1945 could be painted, and briefly describe the main features of that picture.